FUGUE AND FRESCO: STRUCTURES IN POUND'S *CANTOS*

Kay Davis

EZRA POUND SCHOLARSHIP SERIES

General Editor, Carroll F. Terrell

James J. Wilhelm, *Dante and Pound: The Epic of Judgement*

Frederick Sanders, *John Adams Speaking: The Sources of the Adams Cantos*

Vittoria I. Mondolfo and Margaret Hurley, eds., *Ezra Pound: Letters to Ibbotson, 1935-1952*

Barbara Eastman, *Ezra Pound's Cantos: The Story of the Text*

James J. Wilhelm, *Il Miglior Fabbro*

John J. Nolde, *Blossoms From the East: The China Cantos of Ezra Pound*

Kay Davis, *Fugue and Fresco: Structures in Pound's* Cantos

In Process

David Gordon, *Confucius and* The Cantos

Marianne Korn, ed., *Ezra Pound in History*

FUGUE AND FRESCO:
STRUCTURES IN POUND'S *CANTOS*

Kay Davis

THE NATIONAL POETRY FOUNDATION
University of Maine at Orono   1984

Published by

The National Poetry Foundation
University of Maine at Orono
Orono, Maine 04469

Printed by

The University of Maine at Orono
Printing Office

Library of Congress Number: 84-61103
ISBN 0-915032-07-4 cloth
ISBN 0-915032-08-2 paper

The form of the poem . . .
is conditioned by its own inner shape . . .

NOTE TO BASE CENSOR
E. Pound

ACKNOWLEDGEMENTS

Citations to the poem are to canto and page [83/519] in the New Directions *The Cantos of Ezra Pound*. Citations to other material will be found within the text, in brackets if page numbers or multiple citations are necessary. For complete citations, and to acknowledge my indebtedness (especially in Chapter One) to many critical works on *The Cantos*, I include a bibliography. Many citations are to the Pound journal, *Paideuma*, [*Pai*, 6, p. 210] with the author of the article indicated within the text. Two sources (C. F. Terrell, *A Companion to the Cantos*, and Edwards and Vasse, *Annotated Index to the Cantos*) are so valuable that acknowledgement would be constant and unwieldly; although they are seldom cited they were repeatedly consulted.

Parts of the book have appeared elsewhere in somewhat different form. Much of Chapter Five was published in *Paideuma* as "Fugue and Canto LXVIII," and some material from Chapter Three appeared there as "Ring Composition in *The Cantos of Ezra Pound*." An article drawn in part from Chapter One, "Eleusis and the Structuring of the Adams Cantos," appeared in *Contemporary Poetry*. I wish to thank these journals for permission to incorporate previously published material.

I would like to thank John Edwards and William Mulder for their help in my study of Pound's poetry, and the students in *The Cantos* course I have taught at the University of Utah for their questions and suggestions. I am particularly grateful, for advice and help in writing this book, to Carroll F. Terrell.

TABLE OF CONTENTS

INTRODUCTION

This book was written to provide readers with an approach to *The Cantos* through Ezra Pound's own terminology. For example, Pound said *The Cantos* are like fugue, and some of the questions considered here are: What is a fugue? Is one canto like fugue? Or is the entire poem like fugue? And how do the answers to these questions about fugue illuminate the poem?

Most of the words Pound used to describe *The Cantos*, such as *fugue, fresco, ideogram, subject rhyme,* and *arena,* refer to structure, and so this book examines the structure of *The Cantos,* the relationship of the parts of the poem with each other and with the whole, seen through the terms and analogies Pound suggested. Such a study must depend upon an examination of small units, separate cantos and divisions within cantos, and to describe the structure of an 800-page poem in detail might easily require 800 chapters, so I compromise by using early cantos in the first part of the book and late cantos toward the end. In Chapter One, I describe the motion of nekuia/repeat/metamorphosis as a structuring device in Cantos 1 and 2, showing relationships between theme and form. In the next two chapters I describe subject rhyme, ideogram, and ring composition in Canto 6 and in sections from the Adams cantos. Canto 19 and portions of the Pisan Cantos are analyzed in Chapter Four through a study of voice and arena, and in Chapter Five I show how voice in Canto 63 is ordered as a fugue. Late cantos are analyzed in the last two chapters, in which I discuss the Schifanoia Frescoes and the use of all Pound's analogies in reading *The Cantos*. There is reason within the poem for this arrangement. From the beginnng Pound used a system of organization based on subject rhyme, ideogram, and the "nesting" or enclosing of sets of micro-units within a homologous macro-unit; but the late cantos show the use of fugue and fresco much more clearly than do the early ones.

I have assumed that the reader is aware of two of the structuring forces in the poem, the relationship of *The Cantos* to Dante's hell/purgatory/paradise structure in the *Divine Comedy*, and the relationship of separate cantos to decads, and of these decads to the poem as a single unit.

Pound often indicated both the similarity and the differences between *The Cantos* and the *Commedia*, and criticism of *The Cantos* now assumes that there is a general though not a steady motion from a hell, in the first thirty cantos, toward paradise, with Cantos 1 to 30 a hell, 31 to 72 a purgatory, and the rest a paradise. In *The Cantos* Pound has explained that paradise is "spezzato" [74/438], and the poem has "by no means the orderly Dantescan rising" [74/443] of the *Commedia*. Thus there are, for example, moments of purgatory and paradise in the first thirty cantos and moments of hell in the later cantos. As I show in Chapter One, this general motion can be found in individual cantos, and even in smaller units, so that the roughness and "spezzato" effect of the motion toward paradise is due partly to these smaller motions within the short units of the poem.

The individual canto is usually assumed to be the short structural unit of the poem (although I have divided the cantos into "subjects," which are much smaller units) and the separate cantos are collected, especially from Canto 31 on, into "decads" or units of ten or eleven cantos. These decads are a function, partly, of the publication history of the poem, and Pound at times merged them into larger divisions, an organization that can be seen on the "Contents" page of *The Cantos*:

A Draft of XXX Cantos (1930)
Eleven New Cantos XXXI-XLI (1934)
The Fifth Decad of Cantos XLII-LI (1937)
Cantos LII-LXXI (1940)
The Pisan Cantos LXXIV-LXXXIV (1948)
Section. Rock-Drill De Los Cantares LXXXV-XCV (1955)
Thrones de los Cantares XCVI-CIX (1959)
Drafts and Fragments of Cantos CX-CXVII (1969)

The first of the sections, "A Draft of XXX Cantos," might be further divided into decads, including the "palette" of Cantos 1-11 [see *L*, p. 180]. Or it might be divided into Cantos 1-16, 17-30, because the first sixteen were once published separately. Since Pound chose to group them all together in the first version of the complete *Cantos*, I have kept this division in referring to the structure of the poem, thinking of the first thirty cantos as one group, but the later cantos as grouped into decads. There is another instance of Pound's merging decads into one section. He published the Chinese and Adams cantos together in 1940, and although they are clearly two separate decads, they are also quite clearly similar; both were redacted from long histories, both are purgatorial, and both are about the creation of good government. Pound did not include Canto 120 as a separate canto. It was added after his death and in future editions of the poem it may be deleted or its position changed, and I assume that the poem ends with Canto 117 [*Pai*, 11-1, p. 188]. Thus, although *The Cantos* can be said to be grouped into decads, there are exceptions. This organization, like the march from hell to paradise, is not a tidy ordering.

The way to understand the work of a poet, as Pound once said, is to "READ HIM," and I hope that my reader will keep *The Cantos of Ezra Pound* at hand. Although I have tried to quote extensively, in some instances completely, from each of the cantos examined here, such a presentation is necessarily fragmented, calling for a sustained reading of the poetry itself. Even Pound's comments on *The Cantos* (and certainly my comments) cannot be a substitute for the poem each reader must form "in the mind," but I have found, and I hope that the reader of this book will find Pound's analogies and comments compelling; they illuminate his poem.

CHAPTER ONE

ELEUSIS: DESCENT/REPEAT/METAMORPHOSIS

> A real book is one whose words grow ever
> more luminous . . . as one is led or edged
> over into considering them with greater
> attention. . . . Man reading shd. be man
> intensely alive. The book shd. be a ball of
> light in one's hand [*GK*].

A clue to the structure of *The Cantos* by Ezra Pound is given by the dark-to-light imagery of Cantos 1 and 2. This chapter will follow that clue, from the dark/light motion of the rites of Eleusis to the same pattern in the three-part scheme Pound suggested for his poem. Cantos 1 and 2 will illustrate this structure, and other examples from later cantos will show some of the ways Pound varied the subject while maintaining the pattern.

The ancient worship of fertility at Eleusis forms the religious premise for *The Cantos* [see *LE*, pp. 249-275; Surette *Light*], and the dark/light motion of the rites at Eleusis is analogous with the most elementary pattern in Pound's poem, so we will start there, with the myth and rites of Demeter at Eleusis.

The Homeric *Hymn to Demeter* contains the Eleusinian myth, the story of Demeter and her daughter Persephone. Pluto abducted Persephone and held her in his underworld kingdom while her mother, dressed in black and disguised as an old crone, searched throughout the world for her, arriving at last at Eleusis on the fertile plain north of Athens. In her grief and anger with Zeus, who had connived in the abduction, she made the land of the Greeks barren so that many died; then Zeus relented and allowed Persephone to rejoin her mother. In her joy, Demeter taught the Greeks to sow grain, thereby enabling them to settle in one place and "plant" a civilization. Because Persephone ate a pomegranate seed while in the underworld, she was condemned to return there for one third of each year, the summer, which in Greece is the barren time of the year. This means that her return to earth (or rebirth) is a repeated occurrence. Thus the Eleusinian myth is about human and divine sexuality, the abundance of the earth, and the birth of civilization, brought together in a seed motif based on the concept of rebirth.

Each year the rites began with a parade or "pompe" to Eleusis where the two essential events in the rites took place underground. After the participants or candidates descended into an underground chamber they experienced the "dromena," a wandering in confusion, followed by the "epopte," a brilliant light.

The participant in the dromena suffered confusion and darkness analogous with the darkness of Pluto's kingdom, with the condition of the buried seed, and with the ignorance, error, and confusion of the Greeks during the time before Demeter told them how to cultivate grain. Plutarch, in a description of the rites that we believe Pound knew, said the candidate in the dromena stumbled through "chance directions, difficult detours, disquieting and endless walks through darkness." Then, before the end, complete terror; one is overcome by shivering, trembling and breaks out into a cold sweat. Plutarch compared this part of the rites to the life of non-initiates who, unaware of Demeter's grace, "crush and jostle themselves in the mud and darkness, and because of fear of death, remain among the evils from failure to believe in the joy of the beyond" [Surette, *Light*, p. 50].

The climax in the rites was the epopte, a sudden awareness of intense light. Plutarch said of this moment of epiphany or grace, "A marvelous light bursts before one's eyes, and one walks in pure meadows where voices echo and figures dance. Sacred words and divine apparitions inspire a religious respect. At that time, the man, from then perfect and initiated, becomes free and holy and moving about without restraint celebrates the Mysteries, a crown on his head" [Surette, *Light*, p. 50]. Pound understood this moment to be the "magic moment" of orgasm, and he believed that the rites were the worship of "the sexual phenomena whereby Life perpetuates itself mysteriously throughout the universe ... the marvelous vital principle infused by invisible Divinity into manifest nature," a description he translated from the Italian and stressed in "Terra Italica" [*SP*, p. 55]. Our understanding of the moment of epiphany, however, should not be limited to its sexual significance; it also means wisdom or "enlightenment," a worship of Demeter in the abundance of nature, and delight in divine grace.

The Eleusinian rites are implied in the outline of the "main scheme" of *The Cantos* that Pound sent to his father in 1927:

Live man goes down into world of Dead . . .

The "repeat in history" . . .

The "magic moment" or moment of metamorphosis, bust thru from quotidien [sic] into "divine or permanent world." Gods, etc. [*L*, p. 210].

The first part of this scheme is a good definition for the Eleusinian *dromena*; the second element suggests the rebirth basis of the myth, and the final part describes the *epopte*.

The characters in *The Cantos*, like the candidates in the Eleusinian rites, must endure confusion. A few of them, Zaharoff or Hamilton for example, are portrayed as content to live in darkness, or "remain among evils" and manipulate the forces of their own hell (perhaps because of the Calvinistic "fear of death" that Pound hated). Most characters in the poem, however, are purgatorial. They struggle through to attain divine light "if only for a flash" [92/620]. They may err, taking wrong directions or detours that lead nowhere, but even their mistakes can serve as landmarks to guide those who follow. Such a guide is one form of the "repeat in history," and such guides are usually within the dark part of *The Cantos'* pattern, but because of the complexity of the repeat and its constant presence in the poem it should not be identified only with darkness. The *epopte* also recurs. This moment of light (epiphany, vision of the gods, paradise, neo-Platonic *nous*, enlightenment) emerges out of the *dromena* repeatedly. Confusion, Pound said in *The Cantos*, is the basis and source of renewal [20/92, 21/100]. Characters in the poem attain the *epopte* because they have struggled to an understanding of the human world.

This motion from *dromena* to *epopte*, darkness to light, terror to grace, wandering and confusion to the "permanent world of the gods," and human error to divine wisdom is the simplest pattern in *The Cantos*. The simple pattern is then complicated, recapitulated, enclosed within itself. Cantos 1 and 2 exhibit both the basic pattern and some of its complications, and we will look first at the simple dark/light motion, studying the *dromena* of Canto 1 and the *epopte* of Canto 2 before examining some of the more complicated patterns.

Canto 1 opens with a translation of Book Eleven of Homer's *Odyssey*, the journey of Odysseus to the underworld to speak to Tiresias. This is the first part of Pound's scheme, the "Live man goes down into world of Dead," and Canto 1 resembles the Eleusinian *dromena* in its imagery of shadows and "swartest night" as well as its atmosphere of terror:

These many crowded about me; with shouting,
Pallor upon me, cried to my men for more beasts;
Slaughtered the herds, sheep slain of bronze;
Poured ointment, cried to the gods,
To Pluto the strong, and praised Proserpine; [1/4]

Odysseus, like the purgatorial candidate in the rites, insists on learning:

Unsheathed the narrow sword,
I sat to keep off the impetuous impotent dead,
Till I should hear Tiresias. [1/4]

Canto 1 tells this story of the descent into the underworld as if it were physical truth, an immediacy to be repeated in *The Cantos*, most forcefully in Pound's own descent in Canto 82. Characters in the poem will also descend into economic, political, and artistic darkness; the *dromena* in *The Cantos* can be both personal and social. It can also occur in the style of the words on the page. Some of these different aspects of darkness will be described later in this chapter, and Pound's different ways of using them will be the basis for different patterns discussed in the following chapters. For the moment, however, let us pursue the reference to repeated descent as it occurs in Canto 1.

The repeated journey of the live man to the world of the dead, or "nekuia," begins in Canto 1 as Pound is identified with Odysseus. When Tiresias appears he says, "A second time? why? man of ill star," and Odysseus has become Pound.

Furthermore, Pound took this part of his poem from the past, going to Homer much as Odysseus went to Tiresias. Pound believed that Homer had journeyed to the land of the dead for some of *his* poetry, too, incorporating material "from unknown forerunners, short narrative poems, ballads," in his epic poems [*Music*, p. 352], and that Book Eleven clearly came from such a forerunner, now unknown: "the Nekuia shouts aloud that it is older than the rest" [*L*, p. 274]. Thus Pound repeats Homer's journey to older poets for material.

Other poets and wanderers in Canto 1 are part of the "repeat in history." After the translation from Homer, the canto ends with a mix of footnote, other quotations, allusions, and a reference to Odysseus' journey:

Lie quiet Divus. I mean, that is Andreas Divus,
In officina Wecheli, 1538, out of Homer.
And he sailed, by Sirens and thence outward and away
And unto Circe.
        Venerandam,
In the Cretan's phrase, with the golden crown, Aphrodite,
Cypri munimenta sortita est, mirthful, orichalchi, with golden

> Girdles and breast bands, thou with dark eyelids
> Bearing the golden bough of Argicida. So that: [1/5]

Divus translated the *Odyssey* into Latin at the date mentioned, and Pound translated Divus' translation into his own Canto 1. Thus we have, so far, a chain of journeys back from Pound, to Divus, to Homer, to the author of the earlier Nekuia, with each link tied to the Odysseus figure. The "golden bough of Argicida" is a reference to another wanderer, Aeneas, who should be included in the chain. In Virgil's epic, Aeneas found the golden bough in the dark wood near the sibyl's cave and offered it to Proserpine so that he could enter the underworld. Virgil was guided by Homer's *Odyssey*, and he in turn was the guide Dante chose for his own journey from the dark wood through the underworld. Dante was a guide for Pound, and the Anglo-Saxon alliterative metric in the canto is an allusion to other poets from the past who guided him. A final link in this complex chain of repeated nekuias is the reader, who has perhaps gone from Pound's poem to the *Odyssey*, or to a critical work; he too has journeyed to the past for knowledge. The chain will run about as follows, then: Reader, Pound, Divus, (Virgil, Aeneas, Dante), Homer, Odysseus, and the poets of the *Seafarer*, the *Wanderer* and the earlier nekuias. Thus the basic repeat is not Pound/Odysseus; it is, instead, both theme and poetic device, the use of the past as guide in writing of the use of the past as guide.

Canto 2 follows the dromena (nekuia and repeat) of Canto 1 with the epopte. It is about "Gods, etc." and is the "metamorphosis canto," the story from Ovid of a slave ship turned to rocky island, told in imagery of light. Although the metamorphosis is a function of the divine world of Dionysus, it teems with this world's life:

> grapes with no seed but sea-foam,
> Ivy in scupper-hole.
> . . . *
>
> And there was gunwale, there now was vine-trunk,
> And tenthril where cordage had been,
> grape-leaves on the rowlocks,
> Heavy vine on the oarshafts,
> And, out of nothing, a breathing,
> hot breath on my ankles,
> Beasts like shadows in glass,
> a furred tail upon nothingness.
> Lynx-purr, and heathery smell of beasts,
> where tar smell had been,
> Sniff and pad-foot of beasts,
> eye-glitter out of black air [2/7-8].

These are Dionysus' totemic beasts, and the grapes of the god of
wine, but the poetry is homage to the abundance of earth and
recalls the Eleusinian worship of Demeter. There is also divine
love in Canto 2:

> Lithe turning of water,
> sinews of Poseidon,
> Black azure and hyaline,
> glass wave over Tyro,
> Close cover, unstillness,
> bright welter of wave-cords,
> Then quiet water, [2/9-10]

and the permanent world of the gods merges with the earthly
world of abundance to close the canto:

> And we have heard the fauns chiding Proteus
> in the smell of hay under the olive-trees,
> And the frogs singing against the fauns
> in the half-light [2/10].

The perception of sensual human life as divine experience is
Eleusinian, an important aspect of the fertility myth, and it is
presented here in images of light. As the imagery of Canto 1
emphasizes the shadows of the dromena, so that of Canto 2
emphasizes the light of the epopte: "Seal sports in the spray-
whited circles of cliff-wash . . . Spread wet wings to the sun-film,
. . . a tin flash in the sun-dazzle." Because the light is from the
sea as much as from the sun, even blackness in Canto 2 glistens
with light: "eye-glitter out of black air,"and "Black azure and
hyaline, glass wave over Tyro."

   To read Canto 1 as dark only, like the dromena, and Canto 2
as pure light, like the Eleusinian epopte, is, however, to over-
simplify Pound's structuring in these cantos. There is an approach
to the gods in Canto 1, in the veneration of Aphrodite, and there
is both confusion and repeat in Canto 2, so that the two short
dark/light motions of Cantos 1 and 2 are combined into one
longer, more complex motion. Although the allusion to Proserpine
and the veneration of Aphrodite in Canto 1 is muted and cannot
be said to achieve the bright light of Canto 2, it is nevertheless a
release from the nekuia that precedes it. This muted epiphany or
purgatorial rebirth of purpose is rhymed many times in *The
Cantos*, one remarkable example being the "enteuthen [hence-
forth] . . . periplum" motion at the end of Canto 82, as the poet
turns away from his own descent into death towards the "HUDOR
et Pax" or rebirth of Canto 83.

   The "repeat in history" of Canto 2 is an epiphany, at least in
one form, the canto itself. Canto 2 is a repeat of the moment of

metamorphosis; it "makes new" a story from Ovid's *Metamorphoses* and repeats Ovid's stylistic technique of merging one image into another.

But there is also a dark repeat in this canto, especially in the juxtaposition of Helen of Troy with Eleanor of Aquitaine, as Eleanor is referred to by Helen's epithets: destroyer of ships, destroyer of cities. Here, too, is a chain reaching back into time, the Sordellos of Pound, Browning, and the early "vita" for this troubadour:

> Hang it all, Robert Browning,
> there can be but the one "Sordello."
> But Sordello, and my Sordello?
> Lo Sordels si fo di Mantovana [2/6].

And the dark error of the dromena emerges in the avarice of a slaver:

> Mad for a little slave money.
>   And they took her out of Scios
> And off her course... [2/7].

The pattern then for these first two cantos is of short progressions (long-dark to quick-bright in Canto 1, short-dark to brilliantly bright in Canto 2) nested within the enclosing dark/light motion made by the two cantos together. We will find this complication of the simple pattern throughout the poem; it is even suggested by the organization created by the publishing history of *The Cantos*: cantos within decad, decads within poem.

This nesting organization is not the only complication in the dromena/epopte pattern. The "repeat" itself is another because by definition it is a doubling and not a progression; and Pound made the variety, the antiquity, and the recurrence of the Eleusinian theme all part of his patterning. Several of the analogies he suggested for the poem, especially subject rhyme and fugue, are explanations or descriptions of these complications, and later chapters will study relationships between such analogies and the complex patterns. First, however, we might note other ways each element in the descent/repeat/metamorphosis pattern takes shape in the poetry, examining one or two of these, especially the manipulation of opaque and clear style, with some care.

The descent can be a study of history, a period of personal despair or confusion, a record of struggle, a time of social collapse or economic error, or a period of seemingly unproductive artistic work. It can also express itself as obscurity of meaning on the page of the poem, and the consequent search for meaning by the reader. Parts of *The Cantos* are difficult if not impossible to understand unless the reader is willing to do a little research—make the journey to the past. This confusion on the page is immediate, often irritating, and it seems to have been willful on the poet's part. An examination of such a dromena/epopte progression, the opening passage in the Adams cantos, shows that Pound begins with confusion and moves toward clarity, but ultimate clarity depends upon the reader's willingness to go to the *Works of John Adams*, thus making the same journey to the past that Pound made.

The first page of the Adams decad begins with five lines of italics which seem nearly meaningless except as a vague statement of good will:

> *'Acquit of evil intention*
> > *or inclination to perseverance in error*
> *to correct it with cheerfulness*
> > *particularly as to the motives of actions*
> *of the great nations of Europe.'* [62/341]

We do not know the speaker, and we might guess it to be John Adams or Ezra Pound, but in each case we would be wrong. We don't know why the words are in italics as well as within quotation marks, and we might simply decide that the material is in italics because it introduces the Adams cantos, and in that case we would be correct. But the material seems insufficient for this purpose. Why should this nameless speaker *not* be willing to correct his errors?

The next few lines offer glimmerings of sense, torchlight in the labyrinth, especially after the entrance of John Adams:

```
                        for the planting
and ruling and ordering of New England
from latitude 40° to 48°
TO THE GOVERNOR AND THE COMPANIE
                whereon Thomas Adams
                19th March 1628
18th assistant whereof the said Thomas Adams
                (abbreviated)
Merry Mount become Braintree, a plantation near Weston's
Capn Wollanston's became Merrymount.
                ten head 40 acres at 3/ (shillings) per acre
who lasted 6 years, brewing commenced by the first Henry
                continued by Joseph Adams, his son
at decease left a malting establishment.
Born 1735; 19th Oct. old style; 30th new style John Adams
its emolument gave but a bare scanty subsistence.
'Passion of orthodoxy in fear, Calvinism has no other agent
                                                [62/341]
```

The passage is elliptical and confusing but we can discern the Eleusinian themes of planting and civilization and here is some sense of direction, as we recognize names, places, and the evil of Calvinism.

The lines that follow, however, are absolutely clear:

```
study of theology
        wd/ involve me in endless altercation
to no purpose, of no design and do no good to
        any man whatsoever... [62/341]
```

We have moved from confusion on the page to clarity, an Eleusinian structuring.

If, however, the reader does go back a century to Charles Francis Adams' preface to his *Life of John Adams*, he will discover that Pound took his opening lines from Charles Francis Adams' defense of his own scholarship. In this argument, written in third person, Adams explains why his version of history differs from those written about America by Europeans. His willingness to correct any errors may have seemed to Pound to be a "repeat" of the Confucian dicta to leave blank spaces in one's work, for the things one does not know. Here is the passage from the preface, with Pound's excerpts in italics:

> To say that he has acquitted himself of his obligation to his own satisfaction is more than he can pretend. All that he will venture to claim for himself is an earnest desire to be right, and an endeavor by no trifling amount of industry to become so. That he may in many instances have fallen short of his aim will not surprise him. Infallibility in such a department of investigation is altogether out of the question. The writer has detected too many mistakes in his own work, and observed too many in the productions of others, to seek to cherish a spirit of dogmatism. Hence if it should turn out that he has fallen into any essential *error*, or been guilty of material injustice, he trusts that he may be *acquitted of evil intention* in the beginning, *or inclination to persevere in* it against evidence. Should any such be shown to him, he stands ready to acknowledge it with candor and *to correct it with cheerfulness.*
>
> Much . . . new material has found its way to the light, and many old documents have been rendered accessible, which have greatly facilitated the elucidation of important facts in the narrative. The effect has been to rectify many impressions of the events of the last century and of their causes, which prevailed early and have been carefully handed down to us. This is *particularly* true in regard *to the motives of action*, which governed the policy *of the great nations of Europe* during the Revolution, as well as to those which controlled the course of Mr. Adams's own administration afterwards. . . . Yet it is not to be doubted that much material yet remains undisclosed which will still further contribute to a correct understanding of the action of

these times. If the production of it will in any way subserve the
great end of establishing historical truth, it is to be hoped that
no pains may be spared to bring it to the light of day [Adams, C.,
pp. vi-vii].

By journeying to this moment in the past, the reader of *The
Cantos* discovers that Charles Francis Adams' *Life and Works* of
his grandfather is a nekuia for the author, a piece of scholarship
searching for order and light out of confusion. The opening lines
of the Adams decad, like those of Canto 1, refer us to a search
through darkness, "mistakes," "delay," and "disputed questions"
analogous to Plutarch's "chance directions, difficult detours."
There is also a stubborn desire to "elucidate" the confusion, to
"bring it to the light." The reader's nekuia has discovered another,
and the linkage builds, reader to Pound to Charles Francis Adams,
a repeated journey to the past. The repeat also occurs on the page,
as this nekuia at the beginning of the decad repeats the first
nekuia in Canto 1. The "nesting" organization that was noticed
in Cantos 1 and 2 is also repeated here, as muted epopte surfaces
within this dromena passage, metamorphosis suggested quietly
by the change in old world to new, Merrymount to Braintree.

The reader need not make this journey back a century to
Charles Francis Adams' preface. The words on the page will move
toward clarity, as we saw in the Adams statement on his decision
not to study theology, but the reader who does make the journey
will know *The Cantos* in a deeper and more individual way than
the one who does not. He will participate in an act of creation, a
glimpse of "Gods, etc."

The poem's didacticism is rooted in this participation by the
reader. Pound was aware of it and defended it, saying that a "revelation is always didactic" [*L*, p. 180], and suggesting often in *The
Cantos* that his reader should study a subject. He wrote for those
"whose curiosity reaches into greater detail" [96/659], not
erudite especially, but *curious* readers, willing to search out the
facts behind the facts the poem offers. Obscurity or confusion
on the page can seduce the reader into a search for enlightenment,
so that a good book can become "a ball of light in the hand" [*GK*,
p. 55]. It can become a revelation, an epiphany, a guide through
darkness. So, toward the end of *The Cantos*, Pound says of his
own book, "I have brought you the great ball of crystal:/who can
lift it?" [116/795].

The repeat in history may command more of the reader's
attention than either of the other two parts of Pound's scheme
because the poem is itself a guide through the dromena. The
repeat also occurs as subject rhyme, as "palimpsest" and record,

as artistic creation. Allusions to, or names of, human guides are common. Chains of names are common, like this one from the opening page of Canto 82:

> Swinburne my only miss
> and I didn't know he'd been to see Landor
> > *and* they told me this that an' tother
> and when old Mathews went he saw the three teacups
> > two for Watts Dunton who liked to let his tea cool,
>
> So old Elkin had only one glory
> > He did carry Algernon's suit case *once*
> when he, Elkin, first came to London.
> > But given what I know now I'd have
> > got thru it somehow...Dirce's shade . . . [82/523]

This chain carries us back to Walter Savage Landor's underworld; Pound knew Mathews who knew Swinburne who knew Landor. And the Chinese cantos are a chain or epic catalog that moves forward from the time of the myths into the near-present.

Canto 105 provides a good example of several forms of repeat in one canto. Ideograms and words are repeated, and there are translations: "'non spatio, sed sapientia'/ not in space but in knowing." Images, the light looped over Charles' shoulder, for example, are repeated within the canto, as are images and phrases from elsewhere, such as "vagula, tenula." There are quotations from the works of Anselm, a non-ascetic neo-Platonic guide to the *nous*. Anselm believed that God existed because man could imagine him, "not in space but in knowing," and the implication is that this knowing occurs, not by eschewing human things, but by understanding them. There is a catalog of kings in the canto, a chain of political guides who showed economic responsibility, and the repeat here is not only within the chain but in the implied similarity between kings and philosophers: a good philosopher would attain the *nous* because of his understanding of human life, and a good king would be concerned with such ordinary things as the economic health of his people; conversely, a bad king, like a hermit-philosopher trying to reach God by puritanical withdrawal from humanity, might waste the country's wealth (on a crusade, perhaps, as Richard did) while his people starved. The canto closes with another repeat, two poets who direct us away from asceticism:

> Guido had read the *Proslogion*
> > as had, presumably, Villon. [105/751]

Cavalcante and Villon approached light and truth through sensual love and they are linked here to one of Anselm's works on the idea of God as a function of human creativity.

Epiphany in *The Cantos*, the "bust thru . . . into 'divine or permanent world,'" emerges as a lyric passage of poetry, as light, as an image of the gods, and as the act of creation. It is obvious in the intensely lyrical or incantatory sections of the poem that are sometimes cited as excuse for enjoying *The Cantos* in spite of the "prosaic" or "arid" counter-passages. Often these, like Canto 2 for example, are infused with brightness, but light is also a moment of epopte in the prosaic sections; the reference to whale oil light in Canto 69 is an example of this patterning. *Light* introduces one of the longest entries in *The Cantos'* concordance, and reference to *clarity* and *sun* are also numerous. The gods, of course, signal the arrival of the divine world; Aphrodite or Artemis animate many passages in the poetry of metamorphosis. But human characters also glimpse the permanent world. Sigismundo's welcome on his return from Sparta [11/51] is such a moment. The act of creation, either human or divine (or perception because it is a form of creation) is an epiphany in *The Cantos*. Perhaps one of the clearest descriptions of earthly paradise is an "arid" quotation from Brancusi on the process of creation:

> "One of those days", said Brancusi,
>   "when I would not have given
> "15 minutes of my time
>   for anything under heaven." [85/559]

Pound manipulated these Eleusinian dark and light elements into a variety of patterns. He explained the patterns through analogies such as "fugue," or the Schifanoia Frescoes. The next five chapters describe several of the analogies and the patterning each illuminates, beginning with the smallest unit of Pound's structuring, the repeat that he called a "subject rhyme."

CHAPTER TWO

SUBJECT RHYME

> The perception of a whole age . . . into an assemblage of detail.
>
> A set of cubby holes whereinto one can sort one's values and make them into a schema.
>
> The syllogism, time and again, loses grip on reality. [*GK*]

One hazard for the reader of *The Cantos* is the expectation that one subject in the poem's argument will lead to the next in a syllogistic or logical "if, then" way. But the logic of *The Cantos* is to present subjects that must then be related in the reader's mind. The organization seems random but there is a logic which depends upon the reader's recognition of theme, since Pound manipulated the poem's subjects in various schemes based on this Eleusinian dark/light base. In this chapter I will identify the basic unit, or subject, in the poetry, then subject rhyme, and finally the simplest subject rhyme scheme, *abab*, used in the poem.

If we look at the opening lines of Canto 4,

> Palace in smoky light,
> Troy but a heap of smouldering boundary stones,
> ANAXIFORMINGES! Aurunculeia!
> Hear me. Cadmus of Golden Prows!
> The silver mirrors catch the bright stones and flare,
> Dawn, to our waking, drifts in the green cool light;
> Dew-haze blurs, in the grass, pale ankles moving.
> Beat, beat, whirr, thud, in the soft turf
>   under the apple trees,
> Choros nympharum, goat-foot, with the pale foot alternate;
> Crescent of blue-shot waters, green-gold in the shallows, [4/13]

we find a shift of tone and imagery after line two, so that the section divides at this point into dromena, then epopte,—darkness and then light. The first two lines are a glimpse of misery and human error, the Trojan War at the moment of defeat, when we are reminded of the grief of Hecuba rather than of the beauty of Helen or the courage of Hector. These first two lines form a subject, based on the darkness, rape, and murder of war.

The rest of the passage is about light, dancing and music, a glimpse of the world of the gods, fauns, dawn and the birth of a nation. This collection of moments of Eleusinian good might be divided into even smaller units, but it is possible to see the lines as one moment of light, grace, and divinity, a subject representing the Eleusinian epopte, just as the first two lines represent the dromena. The next line in the canto, "A black cock crows in the sea-foam," [4/13] introduces another dromena subject:

> And by the curved, carved foot of the couch,
>   claw-foot and lion head, an old man seated
> Speaking in the low drone...:
>   Ityn!
> Et ter flebiliter, Ityn, Ityn! [4/13]

Here we see human error again. Tereus and Procne had a son, Itys; Tereus raped Procne's sister Philomela, and cut out her tongue so that she could not speak of the rape. Using embroidery, Philomela told Procne of the rape, and when Procne understood what Tereus had done, she killed Itys and served him up as a meal to his father. This third subject, the story of rape and murder, differs from the dance at dawn, and we have the beginning of a subject rhyme scheme, *aba* as dromena/epopte/dromena. Before examining either the idea of subject rhyme or its various schemes, however, other qualities in the subjects themselves should be acknowledged.

First, as suggested in the last chapter, there is a constant nesting organization in *The Cantos*. A unit can often be subdivided into smaller but similar units, and the whole poem is divided into decads, the decads into cantos, the cantos into subjects. As we just saw in the epopte subject above, there could be smaller divisions: Cadmus and the birth of a nation; the fauns of Dionysus; Catullus' marriage song; dawn. These each "rhyme" with one another and, as we will see later, they also form an "ideogram," but for the moment it is only important that we recognize the nesting structure. Thus, instead of saying as I did above that there are three subjects here, we might instead say that there are at least six, and the "rhyme scheme" would then be *abbbba*.

What I call a "subject" might be better referred to as an element or basic unit, or "particular." Hugh Witemeyer, in his article on "ply over ply" in *The Cantos* [*Pai*, 8, pp. 229-235] described this same division of the poetry, calling the separate unit an "element" or one item in a "phalanx of particulars." I use the term "subject" because it seems to me that subject rhyme depends upon this unit, and in turn the entire structure of the poem depends upon subject rhyme.

Whatever it is called, however, we should not assume that each subject is a certain number of lines long, or that it is always an image. Pound manipulates images, ideas, anecdotes, quotations and allusions of varying lengths into his more or less complex rhyme schemes. The nekuia of Canto 1 was one subject, almost two pages long; and each name in the line, "Mozart, Linnaeus, Sulmona," [115/794] is a separate subject. Most subjects can be imaged by the reader, but a few, such as the three names above, work through "logopoeia," the "dance of the intellect," rather than through "phanopoeia," or imagery [*LE*, p. 25].

We know intuitively what a "subject rhyme" is. If two words rhyme because they sound the same, two ideas or images will rhyme because their meaning is the same. When, in the letter to his father referred to in the last chapter, Pound says, "various things keep cropping up in the poem. The original world of the gods; the Trojan War, Helen on wall of Troy . . . Elvira on wall or Toro (subject-rhyme with Helen on Wall)" [*L*, p. 210], we recognize without much confusion what is meant. The two images, each of a beautiful woman on a city wall, seen against the horizon, rhyme much like the sound of end words in a conventionally rhymed poem.

Ian F. Bell has suggested that Pound came upon the term "subject-rhyme" from Emerson or from the Doctrine of Correspondences of Louis Agassiz [*Pai*, 8, pp. 237-239]. Agassiz believed that a comparison of facts would lead to knowledge if one could ignore advice from whatever authority might be in momentary control. *The Cantos'* presentation of subjects without transitions is also a use of comparison without advice. It may be that Agassiz, or Emerson, or some other member of the Agassiz community provided the term, and it should be noted that the *Princeton Encyclopedia of Poetry and Poetics*, under "rhyme," quotes James Russell Lowell, a member of that community, for its one example of subject rhyme: "blue river rhymes with blue sky." Other Pound scholars have assumed that Pound came to the idea from his study of Arnaut Daniel or from Gaudier's "masses in relation" [Kenner, *Era*, p. 93; Grover, p. 134]. On the other hand, it seems to me that although Pound could not be said to write in the early Renaissance rhetoric, especially as that became the "art" Polonius spoke, nevertheless

his poetry is based on the same kind of logopoeia that under-
lies some of the "figures" of that rhetoric as they are described
in Puttenham's *Arte of English Poesie*, written about 1570.
Pound works with synecdoche, "Similitude," and "Dissimili-
tude" [See Puttenham pp. 230, 241; cf *Pai*, pp. 5, 15-29 and
Pai, pp. 6, 13-26]. Many Shakespearean sonnets, like Pound's
poetry, rhyme the three "subjects" of the first twelve lines.

Whatever the source of Pound's subject rhyme idea, however, we return to the fact that we can understand the meaning
of "subject rhyme" quite well. As Walter Baumann said in his
explanation of the term in Pound's letter to his father, "he hit
upon 'subject-rhyme,' implying: You know what a rhyme is,
Dad. Well, in the *Cantos* I do not repeat sounds like 'love' and
'dove,' but I repeat similar subjects [Grover, p. 133]. Whether
because Pound thought the meaning self-evident, or because he
assumed others before him had defined it, he used the term and
the idea often enough to assure us that it was an important part
of his thinking about organization. He said that Munch's learn-
ing-by-doing rhymed "with Dolmetsch's pedagogy for training
children," that Dante's view of rectitude rhymed with Mencius'
view of rectitude, and that the art of allusion in "listening to
incense" was comparable to the Provencal "art of polyphonic
rhyme" [*GK*, p. 248; *SP*, p. 84; *CNTJ*, p. 4; See also 89/596].

Speaking of the way distant pieces of *The Cantos* are drawn
together because they "rhyme," Hugh Kenner, in *The Pound
Era*, said that subject rhyme is the main unifying force in the
poem [Kenner, *Era*, pp. 92-3, 423-7], and I believe that this
is true of short passages in the poem also. Furthermore, I find
Pound manipulating his subject rhymes into complex schemes,
such as the ideogram, fugue and fresco examined in later chapters.
All of these more complex schemes depend upon the reader's
sense of the Eleusinian theme described in Chapter One, and the
easiest scheme to recognize is the simple alternation of dromena
and epopte, *abab*.

Assuming that subject rhyme is the juxtaposition of ideas
that are similar it should give us an "aa" couplet, and, as we will
see in the examination of fugue, this often occurs in *The Cantos*.
If we find an *abab* scheme, however, something dissimilar is
"juxtaposed." Pound often spoke of getting a "cross light" on
something by setting it "against" another idea or subject. Boc-
cherini's music is set against Bartok's, and Landor is "a figure to
put against Voltaire" [*GK*, pp. 123-6, 183, 328; *LBCR*, p. 186].
This juxtaposition of ideas that are different, combined with

those that are similar, can lead the reader into confusion. He can't be sure that the poem is saying one thing or something almost the opposite. The subjects may be juxtaposed because they are similar, or because they are contrary. For this reason exegesis, although vital to an understanding of *The Cantos*, will not help the reader much if he cannot understand the allusions in their thematic context. Conversely, quite often if there is no handy explication of a passage, its meaning becomes clear when the Eleusinian base is remembered; we used very little formal exegesis in seeing the dromena and epopte of the first lines of Canto 4, for example.

I have chosen the following three examples of *abab* rhyme scheme for two reasons. The first is that they are clear examples of dromena and epopte and the second is that each, although exemplifying the alternating scheme of *abab*, also provides a good example of at least one other of Pound's organizational patterns. The first shows the nesting organization, the enclosing of small subjects within a unit. The second uses the "repeat," this time John Adams as Odysseus, and the third is an example of reader's nekuia.

Canto 52 introduces the Chinese and Adams cantos and follows the Siena cantos. It is itself divided into two halves. The first part is dromena, a mix of explanation and invective. It contains two of the most quoted explanations of Pound's Eleusinian theme: "the true base of credit, that is the abundance of nature/ with the whole folk behind it," and "Between KUNG and ELEU-SIS" [52/157, 8]. However, this part of the canto manuscript contained such violent attacks on "human error" that Pound's publishers refused to print the names of the individuals Pound mentioned. He, in turn, insisted that black lines be placed in the text to show this censorship. The result is not only an unsavory violence but considerable confusion for the reader. Thus in spite of references to Eleusinian good, the first half of Canto 52 is confusing and discordant, an intense dromena.

The canto breaks at the words "Know then:" and turns to Eleusinian knowledge:

> Know then:
>   Toward summer when the sun is in Hyades
> Sovran is Lord of the Fire
>   to this month are birds.
>
>   .   .   .

> The green frog lifts up his voice
> and the white latex is in flower
> In red car with jewels incarnadine
> to welcome the summer [52/258]

The knowledge of nature, beauty and creativity is from the *Li Ki*, a book of rites based on Confucian ideas of order, so that Canto 52 moves from dromena and a need for understanding to the good world of Confucius (Kung) and Eleusis.

However, if we examine the last four subjects of the dromena in Canto 52 we find that there are moments of Eleusinian light even here. The passages are about artistic creation, and we will begin with a reference to a painting on the wall of the Palazzo Publico in Siena, "Riccio on his horse rides still to Montepulciano" [52/259]. The picture, as reproduced in *Il Palazzo Pubblico Di Siena* by Cairola [95/101], shows Guido Riccio on horseback approaching a castle on its mountain. Riccio was a Sienese hero, and the Montepulciano mentioned is a reference to the siege of Montemassi. The siege is not as important here as the art, which, like Pound's poem, is constructed of separate blocks or masses,—the horseman, the castle, the military camp. The art, in turn, is not as important as the fact that it has been carefully preserved by many generations of Sienese who care for it. Painted in 1328 (the date is part of the picture), in the age of Dante, the painting still seems new. Its colors are still intense: a Prussian blue sky, black, yellow and red military flags, gold, black and green robes. For its beauty Siena has protected it for six hundred years, and that, as an example of the worship of artistic creativity, is an Eleusinian act.

The next subject, however, is a denial of Eleusinian creativity and abundance, since usury (*neschek*) does not create:

> the groggy church is gone toothless
> No longer holds against *neschek*
> the fat has covered their croziers
> The high fans and the mitre mean nothing [52/258]

This is a description of the Catholic Church after it acquiesced to, and itself committed, the sin of usury. Here the subject is a dromena of human error, darkness that is not a means to light but the result of human refusal to move toward light.

We have moved from epopte (artistic creation and its worship) to dromena (human error), and the next subject will move back to epopte, rhyming music with artistic creation:

> Once only in Burgos, once in Cortona
> was the song firm and well given [52/258]

In one of his reviews of the Rapallo concerts Pound wrote:

> Telemann's music for the *Annunzio a Maria* showed exactly the vigor and fervor that religious music MUST have, and that religion did have in its great days. . . .
>
> Only twice in my life have I heard church music achieve true intensity: once in Burgos, Spain, and again in Cortona, Italy. But it would take too long to explain further what I mean in technical terms.
>
> In this music by Telemann there is real strength. . . . It is an alleluia expressing the exultation of celestial forces. . . . Religion is . . . eternal energy; sometimes even exuberance of energy. This quality is to be found in music, particularly great music, more than in any other art. [*Music*, p. 361]

So this third subject is an epiphany, like the first, and the pattern is now *aba*.

The next subject, which closes the first half of Canto 52, refers again to the groggy church. Like the imagery in most of this canto's first half, the subject is part of the dromena:

> old buffers keeping the stiffness,
> Gregory damned, always was damned, obscurantist.
>
> [52/258]

Pound disliked Gregorian chants, the official church music of the period during which dancing and song were separated from worsip. As the fat-covered vaulting and mitres counter art, so the Gregorian chant counters the "eternal energy" of Telemann's music well performed. This subject, with its "old buffers," also rhymes with the old men on the wall of Troy who distrust Helen's beauty (just as the fat covered croziers rhyme with the raw meat of Rubens) moving far across the poem to link dromena with dromena, the sort of rhyme Hugh Kenner referred to as the main unifying force in the poem. Here they provide the darkness and shadow against which moments of paradise can be seen.

These four subjects form the subject rhyme scheme *abab*, and they are found within the dromena of Canto 52, which could be said to contain an *ab* structure of dromena/ epopte, much as we saw in either Canto 1 or Canto 2, or in the unit made of those two first cantos. In other words, we again have an example of the nesting of smaller units within a larger but similar unit.

A more extended example of the *abab* rhyme scheme can be found in Canto 65, one of the Adams cantos, in which the main epopte references are to the earth's productivity and to the birth of a new nation, rather than to art. There are allusions to other Eleusinian themes such as intellectual enlightenment, and even a few sexual references, but the main thematic references to Eleusis in the Adams cantos are to America and to "the true base of credit, that is the abundance of nature" [52/257]. The negation of these themes is to be found in European corruption, or avarice, or asceticism, the "sin against nature," by which "Stonecutter is kept from his stone/ weaver is kept from his loom" [45/229]. Therefore, in the Adams cantos, John Adams' concern for the fisheries is moral, while Hamilton's interest in money is immoral. Fisheries are Eleusinian, money is not. The nation would prosper in Adams' care and wither under Hamilton's domination, as Spain does under the control of the clergy, in the examples that follow.

Canto 65 contains a series of subject rhymes in which the dromena and epopte alternate, and we can see Pound's use of subject rhyme and Eleusinian theme clearly. This part of the canto is drawn from Adams' diary as he travelled across northern Spain to France in 1779. We break into the canto at a long description of good food, the abundance of the earth, a subject which might be further divided into sub-units, all rhyming on the central theme of productivity.

        pork of this country excellent and delicious
                also bacon, Chief Justice informs me that much of it
        is fattened on chestnuts and upon indian corn
        other pork is they say fattened on vipers
                possible imports to Spain:
        grain of all sorts pitch turpentine timber,
        salt fish, spermaceti and rice.
        Tobacco they have from their colonies
                            as also indigo
        of the King's tobacco they take 10 millions weight per annum
        Saw ladies take chocolate in Spanish fashion
                    dined on board la Belle Poule [65/373-4]

Throughout the Adams cantos we find catalogs of food such as this one, as Adams enjoys European cuisine. In this case we also see Adams' Odyssean interest in practical commerce. What can the new nation trade with the old? How can he nourish America's growing commerce? Like Odysseus, Adams was always conscious of the many peoples among whom he journeyed, and of their economics and politics, as well as their military strength. Like Odysseus, he journeyed far, and for many years was away from the Ithaca he loved and against which he measured other nations. Adams was, in Pound's view, one of the most important leaders of the new nation, if not its greatest, and he was a short, unhandsome, basically honest and forthright man capable of adroit diplomatic maneuvers when necessary. Time after time he was called on to serve America, and at times he gave someone else the credit, if the general good could in that way be forwarded. These Odyssean qualities are often the ones Pound chose for *The Cantos* from the *Works of John Adams* [See also Surette, "Ezra," pp. 438-495].

The next lines in this section from Canto 65 describe the misery of a poorly governed people:

> Galicia, no floor but ground trodden to mire by
> men hogs horses and mules
> no chimney 1/2 way as you ascend to the chamber
> was a stage covered with straw [65/374]

We have moved from Eleusinian good to the darkness of the dromena, but the next lines return to abundance, the seed motif, and a passing reference to Circe's sleeping quarters:

> on which lay a fattening hog
> above, corn was hung on sticks and on slit work
> in one corner a bin full of rape seed or culzar
> in the other bin full of oats
> among which slept better than since my arrival
> in Spain
> [65/374]

The pattern is now epopte/dromena/epopte, and the next lines move us back to dromena, the barrenness of the land as if under Demeter's curse:

> In general the mountains covered with furze
> scarce an elm oak or other tree [65/374]

But that is in turn countered by another description of food:

> O'Brien afterward sent me a minced pie and a meat pie
> at St James Campostella and 2 bottles of Frontenac wine
> [65/374]

Next we move back again to the vice in this corner of civilization that causes the misery, and to the color of Demeter's mourning:

> nothing rich but the churches, nothing fat but the clergy
> NO symptoms of commerce or even of internal traffic
> Between Galice and Leon 1780
> all of colour made of black sheep's wool undyed [65/374]

The alternation of epopte and dromena throughout this section of Canto 65 has made a rhyme scheme of *ababab*, a motion from light to darkness to light analogous to the repeated rebirth of the Eleusinian myth and rites. The repeat, in this case the Odyssean parallel in Adams, also emphasizes this rebirth theme, as we saw it functioning in Canto 1. Canto 65 especially, but all of the Adams cantos to some extent, exhibit this delight in "making

new" the old Eleusinian worship of abundance and good steward-
ship. The theme of the birth of a nation, a making new of the
old Cadmus myth, is a repeat and rebirth, and can be seen as the
main Eleusinian epopte/dromena base in the next section.

In Canto 69, another of the Adams cantos, the intrigue of
the old nations of Europe provides the dromena, and the new
nation's strength and fairness the epopte. We break into the pattern here at the moment of confusion and European intrigue, as
Adams explains in a letter how he tried to obtain loans from Holland and an honorable peace treaty from France and England:

> factions, cabals, and slanders
> many things said to me, false, more I suspect
>   and yet others wd/ do no good if repeated [69/406]

Then Adams is sent to England as Ambassador to the Court of
St. James and, after having lived for many years under threat of
imprisonment as a traitor, he was now summoned to present
his credentials to the king,—a victory for Adams and for America,
proof of the infant nation's strength, and a moment of Eleusinian
pleasure:

> to his Majesty in his closet [69/406]

This is followed by another reference to European intrigue, as
France and England now combine to curb the growth of the
young nation. Adams writes to Jefferson of this collusion:

> To T.J./...of ruining our carrying trade if they can
>   (remaining page ciphered)
> Between St James and Versailles [69/406]

But then in other letters he refers to America's growing strength,
especially at sea, a power that Adams believes America does not
yet recognize, herself. The next lines are:

>   ACT of navigation 12 Car. II, c 18   .
>   navigation by an American master
>   three fourths of the seamen American
>   bubbles of our own philosophical liberality
>   (to Jay, 19 Aug. '85
>   and of the U.S. which wd/ find market in Barbary [69/406]

Next, the poem returns to the dromena, as Adams writes of the
European violation of privacy and the English view of money:

> if both governments are possessed of the contents of my letter
> by opening it in the post office...
>   Mr Pitt said that wd/ surprise
> people here for that wars never interrupted
>   the interest of DEBTS [69/406]

Then, as Adams explains the superiority of American whale oil lamps to the smoky lamps he used in Europe, there is an expression of Eleusinian light:

> Fat of the spermaceti whale
> gives the clearest
> and most beautiful light of any substance known in nature
> [69/406]

Pound clearly saw the young nation as similar to the emerging grain, to the earth's abundance, and to the light of Eleusis, and he set the vigor of America against the corruption of Europe. The pattern of Europe/America, or dromena/epopte, forms an *ababab* rhyme scheme similar to the others described in this chapter. However, there is, at the same time, another pattern discernible here, a much slower motion from dromena to epopte, which can be discerned more easily if we go back to the subject just before those described here.

A subject which describes John Adams' persuasion of the Dutch to recognize the United States precedes the reference to "cabals and slanders," above. This is a moment of Eleusinian good, but it is very difficult to understand without exegesis:

> Nous sommes en attendant charmés de voir
> que les états des autres provinces et conséquemment la
> république entière ont, à l'example des Etats de Frise
> reconnu...
> signed Les membres de la Société Bourgeoise
> de Leeuwarde
> W. Wopkins
> V. Cats
> S.P.Q. Amst. faustissimo foedere juncta
> (on a medal) [69/406]

The announcement, together with a quote from the medal struck for Adams in honor of his success, is to the effect that a new nation has been born. The governing bodies in Holland, having much to fear from England, nevertheless have taken the first step toward recognition of the new nation. The reader of *The Cantos* has difficulty understanding this, however, without a knowledge of several languages and some historical research, so that he is in a state of confusion, his own dromena. The next subjects, also, are difficult to understand, although they require less research than this first subject and they are not written in Dutch, French and Latin. Finally, by the time we arrive at the reference to whale oil light, the words on the page are quite easy to read and understand. There is, therefore, a cognitive motion from dromena to epopte that does not parallel the faster thematic motion. This cognitive motion is similar to the reader's nekuia which we examined in Chapter One.

This combination of structuring forces, rhyme with nesting, repeat and nekuia, can readily be seen in the fairly simple *ababab* pattern described in this chapter; but simultaneity of structuring is constant in *The Cantos*, and even when it is not under immediate discussion it should be kept in mind. When, in subsequent chapters, I describe extremely complex variations of the dromena/ epopte base structure, I will take note of at least two of the patterns, subject rhyme and nesting, we have examined in this chapter. Subject rhyme is the basis for all of the structuring in *The Cantos* with the possible exception of fresco. The nesting organization is the way in which ideogram, fugue, and fresco work. In the next chapter, for example, we will examine one canto, Canto 6, for Pound's use of ideogram, nesting, and the ancient epic form of ring composition. Although the repeat and the nekuia are not really discussed there, they are also part of the structuring of Canto 6. It should be remembered that any structuring devices work simultaneously in each canto.

CHAPTER THREE

IDEOGRAM AND RING COMPOSITION

To make . . .
. . . an altar to Zagreus
Ζαγρεύς

. . .
like the double arch
of a window
Or some great colonnade. [117/801]

My purpose in this chapter is to show at least three structures
working at once in one canto, and to point out that, in Canto 6 at
least, Pound uses a fairly rigid and elaborate form. The complex
and yet nearly perfect ring form, a subject rhyme scheme which
will be identified here, controls the presentation of subjects on
the page in Canto 6. The reader of the canto, on the other hand,
may order these subjects differently; they cluster in the memory
around macro-subjects such as "wanderer" and "property." This
clustering is the result of Pound's "ideogramic method," and in
this chapter the ideogram as structure in Canto 6 will be considered. Both of these structuring devices, ring and ideogram, are
themselves part of the overall nesting pattern in the poem.

Beginning with the organization on the page, we will first
examine Canto 6 as an example of ring composition, a form used
by the oral poets of the *Iliad*, *Odyssey*, *Song of Roland* and
Beowulf [See Niles; Gaisser, and Whitman]. Ring composition
is based on subject rhyme, and in Canto 6 we must examine
Pound's use of "off" or "slant" rhyme, because he does not use
a perfectly balanced form of ring composition, but develops
it through a consistent slant to each rhyme.

Subject rhyme, like rhyme based on sound, can vary in
precision from identity to the "slanted" similarity of "blind
as a bat/eyes floating," a rhyme in which vision is the core of
similarity in both parts of the rhyme, but it is negated in the
first element. Pound used various degrees of subject rhyme,

letting the core idea maintain the rhyme while the ring, or some
other organization of the poem, governed the direction of the
difference or "slant" in the rhyme. Ring composition, even as
Pound developed it, is a closed rather than open form, and the
clearest examples of it are in the very early sections of *The Cantos*,
the "palette," but there are traces of the structure in later cantos,
even as late as Canto 113, where there is only a hint of the form.
I will examine Pound's use of ring composition and subject rhyme
in Canto 6 with some care, then indicate his use of the form
elsewhere in *The Cantos*, after first describing its use in the early
epic poems.

At its simplest, ring composition is a mnemonic device used
by an oral poet. To form the simple ring *abcba* he would speak
first of idea a, then of b, and then of c; at this point he would
either repeat subject b exactly or find a subject rhyme for it;
then he would repeat or rhyme on subject a. If he returned to the
exact wording of a and b, he would have a perfect but repetitious
and rigidly circular ring. If he wished to develop his narrative or
theme he would use subject rhymes for a and b. In an example
from the center of a *Beowulf* ring we can see both repetition and
rhyme:

     Grendel's wish to flee; "fingers cracked"
       Uproar in hall; Danes stricken with terror
         HEOROT IN DANGER OF FALLING
       Uproar in hall; Danes stricken with terror
     "Joints burst"; Grendel forced to flee [Niles, *Beowulf*, p. 926]

The central element, in this case HEOROT IN DANGER OF
FALLING, is called the "kernel" of the form, and its theme
animates most of the other subjects in the ring. The "uproar
in hall; Danes stricken with terror" which frames the kernel
illustrates the use of repeat in ring formation. Usually the wording
itself is almost identical, and we will see Pound using this technique in Canto 4, although not at all in Canto 6. The first and
last subjects in the *Beowulf* ring form a subject rhyme, referred
to by some classical scholars as the "development" of the ring
[Gaisser, p. 4; Whitman, pp. 254-256]. "Joints burst" rhymes
with "fingers cracked" and the wish to flee rhymes with the
need to flee. The narrative is developed, especially in the rhyme
on flight, by the slight differences between the first and second
elements of the rhyme.

The epic poets used "extended" rings, and this one from
Beowulf is only the center of such an extended ring. In some
cases, such as Pound's Canto 6, there is a straightforward ex-
tension of the *abcba* form to ab . . . x . . . ba. In other rings

the extended form may be more complex, containing rings within rings, or chains of internal rings. Both the *Iliad* and *Beowulf* have been described as complex ring structures of this sort, and an example of one such internal ring, a short episode in the *Iliad*, is ab cxc b dyd ba [Gaisser, p. 18]. The epic poets could then both "develop" and "extend" the fairly simple *abcba* form, thereby directing the motion of the poem while keeping the balance and order of the poetic structure. A repeated word might be used to remind the listener of the ring. In the section from *Beowulf*, the word *fleon* is repeated, and we will see that Pound also repeats key words, especially *free*, in the ring structuring of Canto 6, which is both "extended" and "developed."

Here is a diagram of the ring composition of Canto 6. I have summarized subjects and ideas, placing line numbers within brackets. All lines and subjects in Canto 6 are accounted for in the diagram:

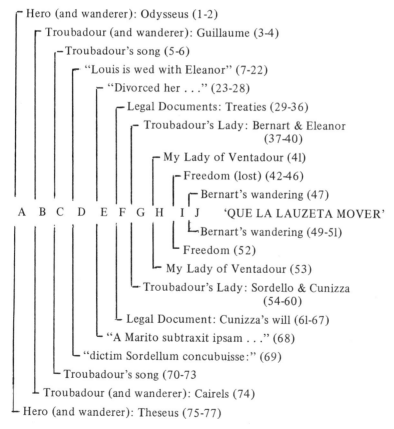

Hero (and wanderer): Odysseus (1-2)
Troubadour (and wanderer): Guillaume (3-4)
Troubadour's song (5-6)
"Louis is wed with Eleanor" (7-22)
"Divorced her . . ." (23-28)
Legal Documents: Treaties (29-36)
Troubadour's Lady: Bernart & Eleanor (37-40)
My Lady of Ventadour (41)
Freedom (lost) (42-46)
Bernart's wandering (47)

A   B   C   D   E   F   G   H   I   J   'QUE LA LAUZETA MOVER'

Bernart's wandering (49-51)
Freedom (52)
My Lady of Ventadour (53)
Troubadour's Lady: Sordello & Cunizza (54-60)
Legal Document: Cunizza's will (61-67)
"A Marito subtraxit ipsam . . ." (68)
"dictim Sordellum concubuisse:" (69)
Troubadour's song (70-73
Troubadour (and wanderer): Cairels (74)
Hero (and wanderer): Theseus (75-77)

When we look at the subject rhymes diagrammed in the ring, relationships that were minor before become somewhat more important. For example, before becoming aware of the ring we recognize the juxtaposition of Sordello and Cairels, perhaps as both obvious and unimportant. They are both troubadours. Reading the poem with its ring form in mind, we can see that Guillaume and Cairels are rhymed, the first troubadour who brought the song up out of Spain, with one of the last, who wrote down the songs of the others. This juxtaposition in the reader's mind of rhymed elements that are distant on the page emphasizes the repeated motion in Canto 6 from the dromena of Eleanor's surroundings to the epopte in Cunizza's section of the poem, the second element in each of the rhymes.

Beginning, then, at the center of the ring and working out to the Odysseus/Theseus rhyme, we will examine each of the rhymes, comparing the first element with the second to see how Pound developed the canto while maintaining its ring structure.

"Que la lauzeta mover," the central subject of the ring, can be translated as "That the lark may move," (or fly) and the sentence that begins with this phrase would read, "That the lark may fly, send word I ask you to Eblis [that] you have seen that maker and finder of songs so far afield as this, that he may free her." Bernart has left Ventadour so that Eblis will free Bernart's Lady (Eblis' wife) from her imprisonment. This gift of freedom will rhyme with Cunizza's will, and the central image of the lark's motion and grace will be reflected in all of Bernart's speech, and in the Cunizza section which follows.

The rhyme (J) on Bernart's wandering which surrounds the central image of the lark alludes to his reason for leaving Ventadour:

"Save in my absence, Madame.

            .   .   .

"Send word I ask you to Eblis
            you have seen that maker
"And finder of songs so far afield as this [6/22]

The freedom of the wanderer is suggested in other sections of the canto, Odysseus/Theseus, Guillaume/Cairels, and Eleanor's journey to Acre, but those subjects on the outer rings of the structure do not emphasize giving freedom to someone else.

The connection between Bernart's wandering and his Lady's freedom is made explicit by the rhyme (I) on freedom:

"Is shut by Eblis in
"And will not hawk nor hunt
    nor get her free in the air
"Nor watch fish rise to bait
"Nor the glare-wing'd flies alight in the creek's edge

. . .
"That he may free her, [6/22]

The rhyme moves from imprisonment to freedom. The first part contains images of freedom in nature that recall the image of the lark, but these are negated. The second half of the rhyme is clearly an echo of that central subject, "that the lark may fly."

Another echo of the image of the lark occurs again in the second part of the rhyme (H) on Bernart's lady, which is first an identification and then a description:

"My Lady of Ventadour

. . .
who sheds such light in the air." [6/22]

The original canto, published in *A Draft of XVI Cantos*, ended with this line, and the only part of that version in ring composition was the speech by Bernart, which we have just considered [Bush, pp. 214-20, 310-13]. Pound added the second element of each of the remaining rhymes and shortened the first part of the poem, eliminating much of the hundred line narrative and almost all of the original emphasis on Richard Coeur-de-Lion. It will be seen that the revision created some confusion in the first section, on Eleanor, so that there is motion in the canto both from possessiveness toward freedom and from confusion toward clarity.

The rhyme on the troubadour and his lady (G) frames Bernart's speech to Eleanor. The first part alludes to Bernart's arrival at Eleanor's court:

Eleanor, domna jauzionda, mother of Richard,
Turning on thirty years (wd. have been years before this)
By river-marsh, by galleried church-porch,
Malemorte, Correze, to whom: [6/22]

The original canto contained more of the narrative here and makes the connection between Eleanor and Bernart's speech more obvious:

E lo Sordels si fo di Mantovana,
Son of a poor knight, Sier Escort,
And he delighted himself in chançons

> And mixed with the men of the court
> And went to the court of Richard Saint Boniface
> And was there taken with love for his wife
>   Cunizza, da Romano, [6/22]

Here, instead of confusion and "Malemorte" we have grace and courtly love.

The rhyme on legal documents (F) echoes the legal phrasing of the original documents. The first part alludes to two treaties, Gisors and Messina, by which the men surrounding Eleanor traded land and dowries, using women as money for acquisition and retention of territory:

> Nauphal, Vexis, Harry joven
> In pledge for all his life and life of all his heirs
> Shall have Gisors, and Vexis, Neufchastel
> But if no issue Gisors shall revert...
> "Need not wed Alix once his father's ward and...
> But whomso he choose...for Alix, etc... [6/21-2]

The original canto contains a reference to Richard's reason for not wanting to marry Philip's sister:

> Richard: "My father's bed-piece! A Plantagenet
> "Mewls on the covers, with a nose like his already." [Bush, p. 312]

and in both versions the theme of war over Eleanor's lands suggests the Malemorte more than the Correze near her court. On the other hand, in the second subject of the rhyme, Cunizza herself creates the contract which gives freedom to the slaves:

> That freed her slaves on a Wednesday
> Masnatas et servos, witness
> Picus de Farinatis
> and Don Elinus and Don Lipus
>   sons of Farinato de' Farinati
> "free of person, free of will
> "free to buy, witness, sell, testate." [6/22-3]

The legal documents are similar in their legal phrasing but the first suggests the hellish "theater of war" [78/477] surrounding Eleanor while the second presents civilization and freedom. The men in the treaty subject trade towns and women; those in the second subject witness Cunizza's act of grace.

Similarly, the rhyme on divorce (E) is slanted:

> Divorced her in that year, he Louis,
>   divorcing thus Aquitaine.
> And that year Plantagenet married her
>   (that had dodged past 17 suitors)
> Et quand lo reis Lois lo entendit

mout er fasché.
. . .
A marito subtraxit ipsam... [6/21,23]

Anger and concern with territory permeate the lines of Louis'
divorce from Eleanor, but the historical violence and war that
surrounded Cunizza's departure from her husband are not mentioned in the second part of the rhyme. The elopement, Sordello's
taking her from her husband, suggests a happy ending to Bernart's love for his lady of Ventadour, and none of the less romantic historical facts are suggested.

The first part in the rhyme on marriage (D) also alludes to
the conniving of the men around Eleanor:

> The stone is alive in my hand, the crops
>   will be thick in my death-year...
> Till Louis is wed with Eleanor
> And had (He, Guilluame) a son that had to wife
> The Duchess of Normandia whose daughter
> Was wife to King Henry e maire del rei jove...
> Went over sea till day's end (he, Louis, with Eleanor)
> Coming at last to Acre.
> "Ongla, oncle" saith Arnaut
>   Her uncle commanded in Acre,
> That had known her in girlhood
>   (Theseus, son of Aegeus)
> And he, Louis, was not at ease in that town,
> And was not at ease by Jordan
> As she rode out to the palm-grove
> Her scarf in Saladin's cimier.

dictum Sordellum concubuisse: [6/21,23]

The rhyme is overbalanced on the first element, a compound
subject made up of Eleanor's marriages and flirtations. The emphasis on marriage, in "had to wife," "was wife to," and "is wed"
is set against Eleanor's promiscuity in "Ongla, oncle," "had known
her" and "she rode out." One effect is of disapproval for Eleanor's flirtations. The original version of the canto [See Bush,
pp. 220, 310] presented her promiscuity as reprehensible only
in the view of the "pouch mouth" chroniclers, and the sense
of Eleanor as "avatar of Venus" is stronger there than in the revision. In the canto as we now have it, the freedom of her flirtations and the wanderer theme of "over sea till day's end" is
tempered by selfishness, irresponsibility, and sulking. Even the
theme of the land's fertility, although it rhymes with Canto 47:
". . . doth thy death year/ Bring swifter shoot?" [47/238]
is here more reminiscent of Eliot's "The Waste Land" than of
Pound's Eleusis. Again, Pound could easily have found selfishness

and conniving in the story of Cunizza and her brother Ezzelino. Instead he presents Cunizza and Sordello as motivated only by love.

The songs of Guillaume and Sordello are subject rhymes:

"Tant las fotei com auzirets
"Cen e quatre vingt et veit vetz..."

.   .   .

"Winter and Summer I sing of her grace,
As the rose is fair, so fair is her face,
Both Summer and Winter I sing of her,
The snow makyth me to remember her." [6/21,23]

They are both troubadour's songs. However, the first, Guillaume's, is the possessive "I had them . . ." while Sordello's song, revised by Pound, echoes the imagery and theme of the lark and of Bernart's speech.

The troubadour rhyme (B) is an identification:

And that Guillaume sold out his ground rents
(Seventh of Poitiers, Ninth of Aquitain).

.   .   .

And Cairels was of Sarlat... [6/21,23]

Guillaume, Seventh Duke of Poitiers, Ninth of Aquitaine, was one of the first troubadours, Cairels one of the last. Guillaume brought the song to France from Spain and lived a free and wandering life. Cairels, because he could not sing well himself, wrote down the songs of the other troubadours and is thus a rhyme, not only for Guillaume and Sordello, but for the printers mentioned near the end of Canto 30.

Finally we come to the rhyme of the two heroes and great wanderers, Odysseus and Theseus, and even here a progression from violence to peace can be discerned:

What you have done, Odysseus,
        We know what you have done...

.   .   .

                        Theseus from Troezene
And they wd. have given him poison
But for the shape of his sword-hilt. [6/21,23]

These heroes are rhymed as free men, wanderers and lovers, all properly part of Canto 6. However, the sirens' song, "We know what you have done," may be a condemnation of Odysseus' piracy. Odysseus was guilty, Pound thought, of the "perfectly useless, trifling, unprovoked sack of the Cicones" [*LE*, p. 212]. Unlike his exploits in bed or at Troy, the sacking of this island was mean, and it would fit with the sack of Gisors and the preparatory skirmishes of the Hundred Years War which fill the first half of

Canto 6. In the second part of this rhyme, on the other hand, Theseus is described at the moment of his homecoming, when his father recognizes him. He has survived the poison of Medea, niece of Circe, and he is young, with his adventures before him.

We have seen that almost all of the separate rhymes of the ring composition suggest a motion from confusion to clarity, or possessiveness to courtesy,—dromena to epopte. The canto itself necessarily follows the same motion, as the confusion and violence of Eleanor's world moves toward the peace and courtesy of Cunizza's. Canto 6 is in turn part of the overall dromena/ epopte pattern of *The Cantos*. Thus we see again the same organizing principle that I have called the nesting structure of the poem. This kind of structuring is also similar to the ring-within-ring form of the *Iliad* or *Beowulf*.

Ring is similar in some ways to fugue, and we will come back to this similarity later in this chapter and again when fugue is examined as a structuring device in *The Cantos*. At this point, however, we should note that the slant rhyme as used by Pound in Canto 6 is similar to counterpoint. A rhyme that points out difference as well as similarity acts like fugal countersubject, which is like, and yet importantly different from, the opening subject of fugue.

Another quality of subject rhyme, one that is almost the opposite of counterpoint, is the tendency toward identification or metamorphosis. If the elements in a rhyme are enough alike they may merge in the reader's mind, creating a metamorphosis, or an intense identification, of the two subjects in the rhyme: Odysseus becomes Pound for some readers; Actaeon, Vidal. Many of the rhymes in Cantos 2, 4, and 7 merge in this way, while others work in counterpoint, so that these cantos are structurally more complex than Canto 6, and the ring form is not as clear in them.

Nevertheless, in each canto it can be discerned:

```
┌─So-shu churned in the sea
│  ┌─Sleek head
│  │  ┌─face of a god
│  │  │  ┌─Naviform rock overgrown
│  │  │  [   GOD-SLIGHT
│  │  │  └─ship like a keel in ship-yard
│  │  └─a god in him
│  └─smooth brows
└─And So-shu churned in the sea, [2/6-9]
```

*

```
┌ goat foot, with the pale foot alternate
│  ┌─"It is Cabestan's heart in the dish."
│  │  ┌ Flaking the black, soft water
│  │  │  ┌─air, air,/Shaking
│  │  │  │  ┌ flaming as if with lotus
│  │  │  │  [    BENEATH THE KNEES OF THE GODS
│  │  │  │  └ set flame of the corner cook-stall
│  │  │  └ This wind . . . Shaking
│  │  └ above black water
│  └ It is Cabestan's heart in the dish
└ Centaur's heel plants in the earth loam [4/13-16]
```

```
┌ blind as a bat
│  ┌─The old men's voices
│  │  ┌─empty rooms
│  │  │  ┌ lone, dead the long year
│  │  │  [   A DRYNESS CALLING FOR DEATH
│  │  │  └ Gone cheeks of the dancing woman
│  │  └─The old room
│  └─The words rattle: shells given out by shells
└─Eyes floating [7/24-27]
```

These diagrams are made up of quoted lines and phrases from the poetry, not summaries of all the subjects in each canto, so that there is material not contained in each diagram. For example, the progression in Canto 4 from dawn to evening is important to that canto's structure and it does not appear in the rudimentary sketch above. I think it is evident that in each case, however, a ring is there as one of the structuring devices.

Two other structures in *The Cantos*, envelope and fugue, are similar to ring compositon. Envelope structuring is the rhyming or repetition of opening and closing subjects, the outer ring of ring form;

> bees . . . chir—chirr—chir-rikk/like the grass-hopper [17]
> ten thousand dollars tew make 'em/ten bob's worth of
>   turquoise [19]
> Between the two almond trees/between . . . two
>   columns [20]
> Who wuz agoin' to stop him!/*you* go and enforce it [22]

Such bracketing may help focus the internal material, as well as link the two elements of the rhyme itself in the reader's mind. Ring composition takes this process a step further, however, focussing the pattern on the central "kernel." Envelope form as Pound uses it is often only a gesture toward such focussing; just as the ring form, as he uses it in cantos other than the one we have examined, is not a rigid form, at times having the forward motion of fugue.

Fugue is much more complex than ring form, but there are some obvious similarities, as well as differences which we might note here. Both use subject rhyme and counterpoint, and the flight of ideas in fugue can return to the opening subject, as in ring and envelope form. However, the rhymes in Pound's fugues proceed in juxtaposition on the page, so that even when a ring seems to appear it is much more general, *aabbaa* instead of *aba*, and in fugue a ring tends to evolve into alternation, *aabbaabb*. Furthermore, fugue uses "voice," and Pound employed different voices in his fugues.

Both fugue and ring composition are organized on the page. Ideogram, on the other hand, is created by the reader who organizes the subjects, not as they are displayed on the page, but as he rhymes and links them in his mind. The "ideogramic method" is a way of writing poetry that Pound evolved out of his study of Fenollosa's book about Chinese poetry and language, [*Instig.*; See also Davenport, pp. 56-122; and Wilhelm, *Later*, pp. 9-19]. Often the term implies imagism, or the use of "concrete" imagery, but since we are concerned here with the structure of *The Cantos*, I will concentrate on how an ideogram is built up out of radicals and how Pound made use of this structuring in his poem.

The simplest ideograms are shorthand pictures of the things they represent. Here is "mouth":

As the idea becomes more complex, or harder to visualize, the ideogram is made up of component ideas, radicals. Here is the ideogram for "bright":

Pound described this ideogram as:

<pre>
              BRIGHT
                    knife
          sun   +   mouth
              fire
</pre>

He then described "fire," the bottom radical as:

resolvable into fire above a man (walking). The picture is abbreviated to the light and the moving legs. I should say it might

have started as the sun god moving below the horizon, at any
rate it is the upper part of the fire sign. [*Instig.*, pp. 41, 42]

Whatever their origin, each of the parts is an ideogram itself,
nested within the macro-ideogram, and they are linked to each
other because each in its separate way directs the reader's mind
toward the idea of "bright." Also, they are linked through their
rhymes: the heat and light of "fire" and "sun" rhyme, as do the
sharpness of "knife" and "fire," and the shape of "mouth" and
"sun." Pound identified "mouth" with "sun," later, in the Pisan
Cantos:

mouth, is the sun that is god's mouth [77/466]

as if the radicals, like connotations, could influence each other.

The nesting of ideogram within ideogram can continue.
The next step is evident in the "rays" ideogram, which contains
as one of its elements the "bright" we just examined. Pound
uses a large "rays" ideogram on page 254 of *The Cantos*, to
introduce the Chinese and Adams section:

Pound's description of this ideogram emphasizes the birds rather
than the "bright" connotation:

RAYS

feathers

bright   +

flying

Upper right, abbreviated picture of wings; lower, bird = to fly.
Both F. and Morrison note that it is short tailed bird. [*Instig.*,
41].

This progression from "mouth" to "rays" provides emphasis.
Mouth has been absorbed into "bright," and "bright" in turn has
been reduced to only one part of the total "rays" ideogram, two-
thirds of which is an emphasis on birds, "feathers" and "flying."

Thus the ideogramic method works to group and grade subjects and ideas, while various forms of pure subject rhyme provide
linear progression. Subject rhyme, even in the circular ring form,
working by juxtaposition of equal ideas, progresses along the
page. Ideogram provides the reader the means to sort and cluster
these subjects in order to emphasize some and minimize others.

The following description of the ideogramic structure of Canto 6 is a result of my own approach to *The Cantos*. In presenting it I have not repeated some of the points already made in my description of ring form, but some repetition is necessary. I have eliminated the use of quotation marks around the names for ideograms.

Canto 6 can be thought of as seven interlocking and enclosed ideograms. The macro-ideogram is of freedom, and it is defined through the wanderer, through love, and through property. Each of these micro-ideograms is then made up of radicals or sub-ideograms in turn. The wanderer is defined through the archetypal wanderer, the troubadour, and the crusader. Love is defined through song, marriage, and the troubadour's "lady," a sub-ideogram that is in turn defined through the archetypal "my lady," Eleanor and Cunizza. Eleanor is herself an ideogram made up of "domna jauzionda," mother/daughter, and wife. The property ideogram (and we have now returned to the three parts of the macro-ideogram of freedom) is made up of crops, dynasty, and the word "acre," which is an ideogram in turn, formed from the town, the measure, and the wildness of the world of Artemis.

This ideogram with its nested sub-ideograms is presented as a chart on the following page. The diagram is not meant to be definitive. Because the ideogramic method takes place largely within the reader's mind, readers will differ in their understanding of and emphasis on various subjects, and thus in the ultimate ideogram. However, I believe this organization accords with the theme as that emerges from the ring form just examined.

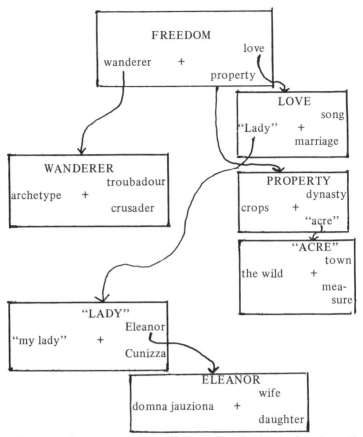

Because the pun on "acre" contains the basic freedom theme of the canto, the idea that people do not own either land or other people, that radical is a good place to begin an examination of the ideogram of Canto 6.

Acre is the town in the Holy Land to which Louis and Eleanor journeyed, and the town where Raymond, Eleanor's young uncle, commanded the crusaders. It is a unit of land measure, and it also means "wild." The *Oxford English Dictionary* contains the following definition among others for *acre*:

> . . . Gr. agros; Skr. ajras plain; originally "open country, untenanted land, forest"; cf. Gr. agrios, L. agrestis wild, agreus a hunter, peragrare to rove;

These words recall the "permanent world of the gods" and Artemis in Pound's poem. Artemis is the guardian of the wild world (see all of Canto 4) and of the outer gates of Eleusis, as Pound reminds us in the first part of Canto 17:

> And the goddess of the fair knees
> Moving there, with the oak-woods behind her,
> The green slope, with white hounds
>   leaping about her; [17/76]

These three meanings for "acre" are linked to the other parts of the property ideogram, dynasty and crops, and to the overall theme of freedom as a result of love rather than of ownership.

The crops radical depends on two subjects. The first,

> The stone is alive in my hand, the crops
>   will be thick in my death-year... [6/21]

identified man with the land and is a statement of the Eleusinian theme, a reminder that life must remain close to the abundance of the earth. The relationship is identification rather than ownership, and this subject is a negation of the usual sense of property. The second subject is the decision by Guillaume to sell his ground rents. If Guillaume did this just before he declared war he put himself in a good position: should he lose the war, the lender would be stuck with the ruined fields; should Guillaume win the war, he would have sufficient loot to pay off the lender. This is, if not outright usury, certainly a non-eleusinian view of land, and it provides the ideogram with a counterview to the identification between Guillaume and his crops.

Peter Makin, in *Provence and Pound*, assumes that Guillaume's sale of the ground rents is a good thing. This, to Makin, is the act of a man who "preferred increasing his knowledge of the world to sitting on acquired wealth." Perhaps Makin is correct. We are dealing with a very subtle distinction, I think, and one that depends on Pound's shifting economic views. However, it seems to me that Guillaume is here being at least as usurious as any lender; he is concerned with the land for what it can bring on the market, not for its produce. While I think Makin is right in saying that Guillaume is "one of Frazer's sacrificial kings, renewing the natural cycle" in the "crops/will be thick in my death-year" subject, I do not think Pound presented Guillaume as, in Makin's words, a "man of courage and developed sensibility." The king who dies may be a king who has failed his people, as well as one who renews "the natural cycle . . . fertilises" [Makin, p. 75]. It is, I think, important that Pound follows the statement of abundance with the word "till." The crops will be thick in Guillaume's death-year . . . *till* Louis and Eleanor are married. If the death-year reference means that by dying Guillaume gave fertility to the land, it is lost again at the wedding of his granddaughter to Louis. Eleanor is traded off as property. She is not a love object but an equivalent to Aquitaine,

Gisors and Nauphal. The manipulation of property often includes divorce, betrothment, or release from betrothment:

> Divorced her in that year, he Louis,
>   divorcing thus Aquitaine.
>
>   .   .   .
>
> Shall have Gisors, and Vexis, Neufchastel
> But if no issue Gisors shall revert. [6/21]

This use of the land and people, trading women, forts and cities, is not part of the permanent world of Artemis and Demeter. On the other hand, Cunizza understands that people are not property; she frees the slaves. Her act is equalled in only one other act in the canto, Bernart's departure from Ventadour:

> "Send word I ask you to Eblis
>   you have seen that maker
> "And finder of songs so far afield as this
> "That he may free her, [6/22]

Thus the property ideogram is made up of a complex of three sub-ideograms, each of which suggests that while man must remain close to the land he does not own it, nor is he the property of another. The land belongs to the gods. Artemis owns "Acre," although Raymond, a man of courage and grace, may command there. Louis, the prime example of dynasty, "was not at ease in that town" [6/21].

The wanderer ideogram is simpler than the property ideogram. Although it is made up of many subjects, none of these is divided into sub-ideograms. There are two archetypal wanderers in the poem, Odysseus and Theseus; there are four crusaders, including Eleanor; and there are seven troubadours, three described and four implied by allusions in the poem: Besides Arnaut Daniel and Bernart de Ventadour, there are allusions to Bertran de Born, and to Cavalcante if "who sheds such light" is borrowed from his *Rime* no. IV [Makin, p. 314]; even Cavalcante's name, which means far-rider, fits the wanderer ideogram. And all of these wanderers suggest that Latin word used by the *Oxford English Dictionary* as a comparison for the "wild" connotation of *acre*, "peragrare, to rove," just as they suggest in many ways the freedom and creativeness of the epopte. However, as in the property ideogram, there is a sense of dromena, too. In the case of the wanderer this means both the darkness of human error, and the confusion through which one must search for knowledge.

Odysseus is the archetypal wanderer and Canto 1 set him in the mind of the reader as the searcher for knowledge, whether or not we believe he was guilty of piracy. Theseus is mentioned twice in Canto 6. First he is identified with Raymond of Antioch,

Eleanor's uncle:

> Her uncle commanded in Acre,
> That had known her in girlhood
>   (Theseus, son of Aegeus) [6/21]

and then he is presented at the close of the poem at the moment of his arrival in Athens, when his father, recognizing his own swordhilt, strikes to the floor the poisoned cup prepared by Medea:

> Theseus from Troezene
> And they wd. have given him poison
> But for the shape of his sword-hilt. [6/23]

Odysseus and Theseus are the myth that is repeated in the crusader, and to some extent in the troubadour.

The crusaders are really Raymond and Richard in this version of the canto (although Conrad was very important to the original version). However, Louis and Eleanor also journeyed to Acre, the crusader's base, so that there is a link between the crusader and the dynasty and "lady" ideograms.

The troubadours are Guillaume, Sordello and Cairels. As we saw, Guillaume and Cairels are rhymed as the first and last of the troubadours. Sordello is also rhymed with the troubadour Bernart de Ventadour who speaks the central quoted poem to Eleanor, and there is an allusion to one other important troubadour, Arnaut Daniel, whose "ongla, oncle" is quoted. The troubadours are not only searchers after knowledge, like the archetypal wanderers (Trobar means "to find"), but they are also creators. They created their individual songs and together they created an age of song. Bertran defines himself as having both qualities: ". . . maker/ And finder of songs."

All of these parts of the wanderer ideogram suggest the freedom theme of the macro-ideogram. Linked as they are to the dynasty and "lady" ideograms, they also suggest the lack of possessiveness that is important to the freedom theme.

The goddess Aphrodite presides over all of *The Cantos*, and somewhere in the ideogram of each canto there is a sub-ideogram for love; and one radical in that ideogram will be the sexual epopte of the Eleusinian rites, caught here in the line, "dictum Sordellum concubuisse" and seen also in the repeated marriages of the first part of the canto. The other two sub-ideograms to love in Canto 6 are the songs of the troubadours and the troubadour's "lady."

Poetry and song by Guillaume, Arnaut Daniel, Bernart de Ventadour, Cavalcante, and Sordello, as well as Pound's early poetry and the canto itself make up the song ideogram. Some is randy, some courtly, but all is love poetry, with the possible exception of the allusion to Pound's translation of Bertran de Born's lament for the death of the young king. Guillaume's "fucked them, as you will hear, 100 + 4 x 20 + 8 times" [*Com.*, p. 23] rhymes with Arnaut Daniel's song of the nail and uncle, and both are set against the Bernart's song of the lark and Sordello's "Atretan deu ben chantar." Pound has rewritten all of these, turning them to his own use in a song about love and freedom.

The "lady" ideogram contains sub-ideograms that are themselves complex, as the chart shows. The basic three, Eleanor, Cunizza, and the "lady" as seen in Bernart's lady as well as in Alix, can each be thought of as composed of radicals such as Cunizza's gift of freedom, but I will analyze only the extremely complex Eleanor ideogram.

At her most paradisal the lady is, like Beatrice, the object of worship; she is also Demeter/Persephone and Aphrodite. Canto 6 constantly sets this ideal against woman-as-property, as we have seen in examining the dynasty ideogram. While the lady ideogram contains both of these aspects, it is not a simple "setting against" of dromena and epopte. There is a complex combination of many qualities, most tied up in Eleanor's character, and all of them important to *The Cantos* as a whole. "Woman" in *The Cantos* changes from this romantic "lady"/property idea to the beautiful, wise, and worshipped queen of the Thrones decad.

The lady of Ventadour is loved by Bernart who has written poems to her. She is also Eblis' property, and Eblis has imprisoned her. Alix, too, is property. She is Richard's "father's ward," and her relationship to the dynasty ideogram is clear. Richard "need not" marry her since she became of no value once his father begot a Plantagenet on her. Although she does not seem to be a troubadour's lady, her situation rhymes with that of the lady of Ventadour, and with Eleanor's condition in Canto 7 where she is "spoiled in a British climate" after her imprisonment by Henry. Cunizza seems to be the opposite of this, a lady loved by Sordello and able to grant freedom to others. She is clearly a forerunner of the good women of the later cantos. Eleanor is a little of both, and her mother/daughter relationship is also emphasized in Canto 6.

A different macro-ideogram can appear in Canto 6 to another reader, but it would not be greatly different. For example, Guy Davenport sees the ideogram of the canto as the siren's song, or the conflict between luxury and will, noting such sub-ideograms as "acre" and "domna jauzionda" [Davenport, p. 276]. There is not a wide difference between his ideogram and the one for freedom that I have suggested, and we would not expect too great divergence if the ideogramic method works. However, one hazard in the method is the possibility of judging or measuring an ideogram against the theme. This is the basis of the different views of dynasty that Makin and I hold; he believes that Pound thought highly of dynasties (a function of Pound's fascism) but I believe that Pound thought highly of dynasties if they "linked" back to Eleusinian truth, not if they were an impediment to truth. The American cantos are poems in honor of the breaking of dynasties.

Whether or not either ring form or ideogram works well is dependent on the reader's willingness to read the poem as a series of subjects. Neither method will work and the structure in *The Cantos* will have no use for the reader if he cannot approach the poetry in this way. However, once that step is taken, it seems to me that the structures are there and that they are of assistance in reading and understanding the poetry. Furthermore, they add to the delight of the poetry, a pleasure that increases as we move toward the later cantos, and the rhymes that link the poem together become more complex and the meanings deeper.

Organization through ideogram occurs in each canto of the poem, but Pound did not again use ring composition as rigidly as in Canto 6, perhaps because the ring does not provide sufficient linear movement, even when it is developed through slant rhyme. Each canto, if dependent upon ring (which circles back on itself) and ideogram (which groups or clusters the ideas) would become autotelic, a window mirroring itself, and "the great colonnade" could not be joined. Fugue provides better linear structure and Chapter Five will describe Pound's use of fugue. First, however, we should examine Pound's use of "voice" and "arena," two devices for helping the reader distinguish subject.

CHAPTER FOUR

ARENA AND CONVERSATION

> . . . the drama was wholly
> subjective [74/430]

> And we sit here...
> there in the arena... [4/16]

> . . . Ford's conversation was
> better,
> consisting in *res* non *verba* [82/525]

Pound used staging and voice as devices for enclosing and for distinguishing subjects, and Canto 19 is a good specimen for the study of these devices because it contains complex scenes and clear shifts in voice. It is also a good example of a rhyme pattern that has moved away from the formal ring composition of Canto 6 toward fugue.

Although distinction and transition between subjects are the responsibility of the reader, the poem offers clues. There will be sometimes, if not often, a stanza division,—white space on the page. Or there will be a very clear shift of idea: "Art is local,/ Ike driven to the edge, almost, of a thought" [97/678]. More often, type or punctuation offers a signal: italics, a period, or parentheses. However, the best clues are a result of imagery and voice. By juxtaposing image and sound as if presenting them on a stage or screen, *The Cantos* "stages" a subject, and Pound refers to the "arena" several times in the poem, as if to remind his reader of this staging process:

> And we sit here...
> there in the arena... [4/16]

> And we sit here
> under the wall,
> Arena romana, Diocletian's, les gradins
> quarante-trois rangées en calcaire. [12/53]

And another day or evening toward sundown by the arena
(les gradins) [29/145]

So we sat there by the arena, [78/481]

The arena is a round stage, originally covered with sand, on which
acting or conflict takes place, and Pound tells us that we are sitting on the steps, "les gradins" looking down at events on that
stage. The Theatrum in Diocletian's Baths, constructed in the
early fourth century, is given by the *Index* as the specific allusion for all arena references. However, any stage, even the modern
cinema or TV, could apply because the poem uses montage,
a cinematic device of throwing one image after another onto
the mind without narrative or logical transition, often repeating one or more important images [*Pai*, 6, pp. 185-232].

At its simplest, this staging process depends on the use of one
static image for each subject. One image is presented, then another:

> as the young lizard extends his leopard spots
>   along the grass-blade seeking the green midge half an ant-size
> and the Serpentine will look just the same
> and the gulls be as neat on the pond
> and the sunken garden unchanged
> and God knows what else is left of our London
>   my London, your London
> and if her green elegance
>   remains on this side of my rain ditch
>   puss lizard will lunch on some other T-bone
>
> sunset grand couturier. [80/516]

First an image of the lizard ready to pounce on a midge is
flashed onto the screen. Next we are shown the Serpentine
in Hyde Park, then gulls on a pond, then a sunken garden. These
three images are rhymed as belonging to London in the next two
lines. Then the image of the lizard is repeated, but this time
with a wider frame, so that we also see the ditch around Pound's
tent. Finally, there is the sunset. Each of these images works
within Canto 80 and within the Pisan Cantos in many ways.
For example there are rhymes back to the Plantagenets, and
forward to Paquin. First, however, they are rhymed here as
moments of natural beauty in man-made London and the de-
tention camp. Pound once said that "the image itself is the speech"
[Grover, p. 23] and these images speak of man's relationship
to nature and beauty. The reader must note the rhymes and the
connections, provide the reasoning and the transitions, but the
speech is there in the imagery.

In this instance it is not very difficult to distinguish the almost static image of the lizard from that of the gulls. However, Pound often set more complicated subjects next to equally complex images or scenes so that the reader's job is made more difficult. Pound would then further complicate his subject by adding characters, conversation, and motion. Conversation was particularly important to him because the exact words, like an image, could provide the poem with reality, cadence, and a device for distinguishing one structuring element from another.

When Pound uses John Adams' words or a quotation from Dante, he is using voice as if it were an image. For this reason, almost all of the foreign language in the poem is quotation. Both imagery and voice are in this sense an attempt to present the *res*, the thing itself, and natural speech could also provide a true cadence with which to supplant the conventional pentameter. His advice to students and young poets who wrote to him was to use the "live phrase" of the spoken language. At one point he quoted from Shakespeare:

> "Faith . . . she would serve, (pause)
> After a long voyage at sea." [*L*, p. 299]

and said, "cadence is so well-taken that even the archaism in the first word doesn't dim the naturalness of the sentence" [*L*, p. 299]. Pound would practice his lines on his friends, to get the feel of his audience's response. William McNaughton describes him trying out lines from the cantos on visitors at St. Elizabeth's [*Pai*, 3, p. 323], and Pound's daughter tells of her father composing in

> a kind of chant that sometimes went on for hours, interrupted and picked up again, no matter whether he was sitting at table or walking in the streets. Hard as I tried to imitate this humming, I never could. No words: sounds bordering on ventriloquism, as though some alien power were rumbling in the cave of his chest in a language other than human; then it moved up to his head and the tone became nasal, metallic. [Rachewiltz, *Disc*, pp. 46-47]

Alluding to the nekuia, David Gordon describes the effect of these practice runs on the audience: "a ghost would speak through the voice of a living man. It made your hair rise to hear him bring back the dead" [*Pai*, 3, p. 352].

It is not surprising then that Pound enjoyed Landor's imaginary conversations or that he wrote some of his own [*ABCR*, p. 186]. Most talk, like these imaginary conversations and like dialogs, even those of Plato but especially those of Dryden and Eliot, are non-syllogistic. Many answers are presented and the right one, when and if it is offered, is reduced to equality with all the others. Ideas are juxtaposed. Conversations would thus be a very attractive device for the writer of *The Cantos*, fitting comfortably with subject rhyme and a speech of images.

Furthermore, voice could be used to cue the reader, helping him distinguish one subject from another. Pound once wrote to his father, "As to Cantos 18-19, there ain't no key. Simplest parallel I can give is radio where you tell who is talking by the noise they make [*Pai*, 8, p. 382]. This structuring device is used with subtlety and power in the Pisan Cantos, where voice is a means of recalling the *res*, controlling the cadence, and distinguishing one idea and one pattern from another. Voice is perhaps not as adeptly controlled in the early cantos Pound wrote his father about as it would be later in the Pisan Cantos. Nevertheless, Canto 19 is a good example both of voice and staging, and its lack of subtlety may make it an easier specimen to examine for this purpose.

I find the ideogram for Canto 19 to be the early twentieth century's failure to keep the peace. The subideograms are:

(a) *The restraint of freedom*, especially the freedom of communication, and the distribution of ideas, goods, and credit. Coal must move through Diamond Jim's hands so he can get his $2.00 cut, and hemp must go through Rotterdam. An economics of scarcity is imposed on inventors and creative people who need credit to distribute their creations. Communication is restrained. The "slick guy" doesn't read the gossip newspaper, and the telephone doesn't work. Most important, economic truth can't be explained to the revolutionaries:

> "Can't move 'em with a cold thing, like economics." [19/85]
>
>   .   .   .
>
> "No use telling 'em anything, revolutionaries,
> Till they're at the *end*,
> Oh, absolootly, AT the end of their tether. [19/86]

(b) *Armchair diplomacy*. Slender "diplomatdentists" wearing roses in their button-holes have not kept the peace. They do not suffer from the war, however, but remain safe "through the whole bhloody business" [19/85]. Their diplomacy is described:

> "So there was my ole man sitting,
> They were in arm-chairs, according to protocol,
>
>   .   .   .
>
> And he knew, and they knew, and each knew
> That the other knew that the other knew he knew, [19/87]

This power to control events then passed to the hands of revolutionaries, the basis for the third sub-ideogram in the canto.

(c) *The birth of a nation.* Three revolutions are alluded to or described, the Irish, Mexican, and Slovakian. There is also a line near the center of the canto, "Short story, entitled, the Birth of a Nation" [19/85] which has been read as a reference to the Russian Revolution, but it may instead be a summing up of the three other examples of twentieth-century revolution.

None of these national births is treated with the respect Pound accords the American Revolution and John Adams, however. In fact, Canto 19 is almost entirely dromena, and it is a darkness of human error more than of a search for truth, although both elements are there. There is no clear sense of a motion from hell toward paradise, and even the faint glimmerings of epopte are muted, as in the reference to the kindly professor.

I examine the first few subjects, which introduce the three sub-ideograms, with some care for their use of staging and voice. I then list all of the subjects, showing how they rhyme and indicating voice shifts.

The first scene in the Canto shows the power of ten thousand dollars. The inventor can't get his invention distributed, but he can sell it, because he can threaten to distribute it himself:

> Sabotage? Yes, he took it up to Manhattan,
> To the big company, and they said: Impossible.
> And he said: I gawt ten thousand dollars tew mak 'em,
> And I am a goin' tew mak 'em, and you'll damn well
> *Have* to install 'em, awl over the place.
> And they said: Oh, we can't have it.
> So he settled for one-half of one million.
> And he has a very nice place on the Hudson,
> And that invention, patent, is still in their desk. [19/84]

The inventor threatens to sabotage "them," and they in turn would sabotage him, if he did not have the ten thousand dollars. But, more importantly, the free distribution of ideas and creativity has been restrained, and abundance of the earth has been sabotaged.

The subject is not presented with the intense clarity of the lizard image, and the voice shift between characters is more noticeable than the images we get of the Hudson or of the meeting. The account is presented by a controlling voice (a narrator or interlocutor or anchorman) and then we hear the voice of the inventor himself, then the spokesman for business. The inventor has the accent that in Pound studies is referred to as "cracker-barrel" American: "I gawt . . . tew . . . awl over." The reader may well hesitate over how to pronounce "mak" but otherwise the clues to the speech are in the spelling, and the inventor's voice seems distinct. It differs from the narrator's voice, which is closer to standard American or perhaps somewhat British; "Oh, we can't have it." However, in the next line, presumably spoken by the same narrator about the same subject, "And the answer to that is: Wa'al he had the ten thousand," the narrator may be quoting the inventor, or he may have picked up the inventor's crackerbarrel voice, an error eschewed even by hack writers of escape fiction.

The second subject rhymes with the first. Old Spinder also has money enough so that, like the inventor, he does not need to depend on credit. However, we don't see him. Instead, we see a speaker, presumably the narrator. The narrator's voice moves toward pure crackerbarrel from standard American, perhaps because we see him at two times, when he tells the story, and the time in his youth when he spoke to Old Spinder. At first he speaks much as he did early in the first subject:

> And old Spinder, that put up the 1870 gothick memorial,
> He tried to pull me on Marx, and he told me   — —
> About the "romance of his business":
> How he came to England with something or other,
>   and sold it.
> Only he wanted to talk about Marx, so I sez: [19/84]

Now he acquires a voice more like the inventor's:

> Waal haow is it you're over here, right off the
>   Champz Elyza?
> And how can yew be here? Why don't the fellers at home
> Take it all off you? How can you leave your big business? [19/84]

Then old Spinder answers in the narrator's crackerbarrel voice:

> "Oh," he sez, "I ain't had to rent any money...
> "It's a long time since I ain't had tew rent any money." [19/84]

And the narrator comments:

> Nawthin' more about Das Kapital,
> Or credit, or distribution.

There may be some distinctions here between voices. The narrator doesn't use "ain't," for example. There seems to be a different narrator for the Irish revolutionary scene, while Lincoln

Steffens is to some extent the narrator for the Mexican revolution, so that there is some distinction later in the Canto. However, it doesn't seem to me that voice is used efficiently.

Efficiency in structuring is not of paramount importance,
however, and voice has other uses. For example, the "good guys"
in this canto tend to speak American, so that the inventor, the
narrator, and Steff (Lincoln Steffens) are allied against the "slick
guy" and other restraints on freedom.

The next two subjects are much more like the simpler images
of lizard and gulls that we looked at first. Also, the English and
French voices which speak these vignettes are very clear. The
English voice tells of the dilettante:

> And he "never finished the book,"
> That was the other chap, the slender diplomatdentist [19/84]

The French emphasizes the diplomat's effeminacy:

> Qui se faisait si beau. [19/84]

The fifth subject introduces the "birth of a nation" theme
with an allusion to the Irish revolution. Like the first two subjects, this is a narrative which coheres as one subject and yet contains separate images, characters and actions. These alternate in
a *cacac* scheme, so that the revolution is played off against the
restraint of freedom theme, the restraint of communication especially. This alternating scheme seems to me to be enclosed within
a rhyme that I identify as (a'). In the "old kindly professor"
we have a glimpse of epopte, one of the few in this canto and the
light here is not particularly brilliant. This subject rhymes with the
invocation to the muse of history in that both of these elements,
unlike the other (a) elements, suggest communication accomplish-
ed instead of human error and restraint of freedom.

So we sat there, with the old kindly professor,	(a')
And the stubby little man was up-stairs.	(c)
And there was the slick guy in the other	
corner reading The Tatler,	(a)
Not upside down, but never turning the pages,	
And then I went up to the bed-room, and he said,	(c)
The stubby fellow: Perfectly true,	
"But it's a question of feeling,	
"Can't move 'em with a cold thing, like economics."	(a)
And so we came down stairs and went out,	
And the slick guy looked out of the window,	(c)
and in came the street "Lemme-at-'em"	
like a bull-dog in a mackintosh	
O my Clio!	(a')

[18/84-85]

The "stubby little man" is identified by the *Companion* as Arthur Griffith, leader of the Irish Sinn Fein, and he represents the Irish revolution here. The slick guy is a police spy and holds but does not read *The Tatler*. He seems to unleash the dogs of war. Scenes having to do with communication are alternated with scenes about the Irish revolutionary, and there is an alternation, too, between upstairs and down. There is only one narrative, however, and it, together with its afterthought about the telephone, are bounded by white space on the page.

The staging of this small drama, like the staging of most of Canto 19, seems to me to work fairly well, although research is needed in order to recognize some of the characters and incidents. The characters have a faceless quality. Unlike a Borgia or a Thomas Jefferson, pictures of early twentieth-century figures such as Prishnip or Lincoln Steffans do not immediately come to mind. However, their very anonymity adds to the general image of gray hell in this canto, in which even the Mexican scenes seem to take place under a heavy overcast.

On the other hand, it seems to me that Pound has misused voice, in spite of, or perhaps because of, his emphasis on it here. I think Canto 19 fails partly because voice, even in this imagist's poem, *is* the poetry. No one has claimed that Canto 19 is an intensely lyric poem. It is a description of twentieth-century hell, not magnificent in evil but terrifying in its grubbiness and in the power of the squalid. Prishnip, whom no one would draft into any army, triggered the bloodiest war yet known, and it is Prishnip that we see in Canto 19, not the evil glory of the Marne boneheap. Pound's hell is never glorious. But both usury cantos speak of human error and in them voice is used with subtlety. If the King James version of the Old Testament is recognized, it is worthy of the allusion and it supports the theme. But in Canto 19 the voice does not ring true and it is not worth attending to. It is not the *res* and it says too little. Although cadence and humor might be gained by the crackerbarrel voice, its purpose seems mainly structural. It is the "noise" by which we are to determine subject shifts. Instead, it should be the noise the poem is.

Furthermore, I don't believe voice does a very good job at this structuring in Canto 19. I list below all of the subjects in this canto, with their subject rhyme schemes on the left. The restraint of freedom theme is identified as *a*, armchair diplomacy as *b*, and the birth of a nation as *c*. On the right I have identified the voice in each subject as I hear it. I do not hear any very distinctive voice in most of the subjects after the first few:

a	Invention stopped	Crackerbarrel/American
a	Credit stopped	Crackerbarrel/American
b	Diplomat	English
b	Diplomat	French
c	Revolutionaries/ Communication	American or English
a	Telephone stopped	American
c	Revolution/War (assassination)	American or English
c	Slovakian Revolution	English with accent
b	Vlettman	American
c	Vlettman/Slovakian Rev	English
c	Slovakian Revolution	American
c	Short Story/Birth of Nation	American
b	Diplomat/rose	American or English
b	Diplomat/war	American or English
a	Goods: naptha	American
a	Goods: hemp	American
b	Armchair diplomat/Albert	German
b	Armchair diplomats	American
c	Revolution/ Communication	American
c	Mexican Revolution	American
a	Coal/Mortgage	American
a	Coal/Diamond Jim	American
b	Armchair diplomats	American
b	Albert	American
a	Ten years taken	English
a	prostitution	English
a	Prostitution	American?
a	Goods: ten bobs worth	English

This list of subjects in Canto 19 points out a pattern that is more interesting than the use of voice as a structuring device, however. Canto 19 suggests both ring form and fugue. Although it begins and ends with a rhyme, and contains some short ring forms (ten years/prostitution/prostitution/ten bobs worth, or Albert/diplomats/diplomats/Albert) the pattern is not the clear ring compositon of Canto 6. On the other hand, although the scheme here is a series of couplets similar to the subject/answer of fugue, the random weaving of the three themes is not yet the

flight of episodes around a central theme that we will find in
the fugue discussed in the next chapter. Canto 19, however, is
very much like the later cantos in its approach to fugal patterning.

Conversely, the Adams cantos, which provide good examples
of fugue, can also be seen as dialogs, conversations, or as staged
dramas such as those we see in Canto 19. In the Adams cantos,
however, Pound made a more subtle use of voice, and he used
Adams' own words as the real image.

CHAPTER FIVE

FUGUE

some minds take pleasure in counterpoint
pleasure in counterpoint
[79/485]

Pound spoke and wrote to several people about the analogy between fugue and *The Cantos*, describing the scheme of the poem as similar to the theme/response/counter-subject of fugue. For example, in 1927 he mentioned this analogy to his father, and ten years later he wrote John Lackay Brown, "Take a fugue: theme, response, contrasujet . . . *The Cantos* are in a way fugal," and then, about five years later, he repeated the idea to his daughter [*L*, pp. 210, 294; Rachewiltz, *Disc.,* p. 159]. If we assume that he meant what he said, it ought to be possible to discover the pattern of a fugue in a single canto, or a single decad; and, in fact, the Adams cantos, written in 1939, do exemplify the importance of Pound's concern with fugue during the 1930s, the Rapallo music years. I have examined the Adams cantos in terms of fugue, and a pattern like that of fugue's theme/response/counter-subject is in each of these cantos and also in the Adams decad as a whole. Canto 63 is an excellent example of this use of fugue as a way of structuring.

In order to explain how fugue works in Canto 63 and in the Adams decad, I will first describe fugue, using illustrations from music, from Pound's poem and his poetic juxtaposition, and from his own definitions of musical fugue. Then I will trace Pound's comments on the analogy between *The Cantos* and fugue, and the comments made by critics on this subject, from 1927 up to the present. Finally, I will examine Canto 63, voice by voice, in terms of the theme/response/counter-subject of fugue, as well as other devices from musical fugue, such as episode, inversion, and stretto.

Pound preferred polyphonic music, the kind written by Bach and Vivaldi, to what he called the "soupy chords" and "sloppiness" of nineteenth-century music [*GK*, p. 252; *Music*, p. 459]. In polyphonic music the different voices or strands are linear and can be heard separately. Contrapuntal music is polyphonic music in which one strand contrasts with the other(s). Fugue, which means "flight" from the Latin for "to flee," is a short piece of contrapuntal music around one theme. The basic elements of this chase, or flight, are theme/response/counter-subject (or subject/ answer/counter-subject).

First let us look at *theme/response* (or *subject/answer*). Here are the first four bars, without counter-subject, of Bach's Fugue 2 from Volume I of the Welltempered Clavier:

The first voice, on the lower staff, gives us the *theme*, or *subject*. This is both a pattern of notes and an idea. When it is complete, the second voice repeats the same theme (or subject, or pattern) but at a higher pitch. This is the *response*, or *answer*. The relationship between subject and answer is that of subject rhyme, and it will be seen that the basic units for Pound's fugues are the same subjects we have studied in ring composition and other forms of subject rhyme.

The *counter-subject* is the juxtaposition of ideas that are different. When we looked at the first four bars of Bach's fugue, we saw only the theme/response. The counter-subject was taken out. Here are the same four bars, showing the counter-subject:

After opening the fugue with the subject, the first voice continues with the counter-subject, while the second is giving us the response. The counter-subject is not the same pattern. It is related to the subject, but it often moves "counter" to it. Notice that in music the two voices are heard simultaneously. This won't occur, of course, in Pound's poetry; his counter-subject will follow the response instead of being heard simultaneously with it.

As in music, Pound's counter-subject will be related to the subject, and differ from it. The idea itself is different, and the voice may (or may not) differ from the voice that spoke the theme. In Canto 63 Charles Francis Adams' voice introduces both the subject and the first counter-subject ("change"), but Pound's own voice introduces the second counter-subject ("learning").

These three elements, theme/response/counter-subject, are usually at the center of Pound's remarks on the analogy between his poem and fugue. They are the means he uses in his patterning of the juxtaposed similarities. But there are other devices used in musical fugue that we should look at before going on to either Pound's remarks on the analogy, or to the examination of the analogy in Canto 63. Three of these devices are episode, inversion, and stretto.

An *episode* can be used to link the strands of theme and it can be an important part of the contrapuntal web that makes up the middle section of a fugue. The musician can manipulate episodes, theme, and counter-subject to increase interest as the fugue progresses. This two-bar episode is from Bach's Fugue 2:

Notice that this does not contain the subject/answer, or subject-rhyme organization that the opening four-bar example contained. Musical episodes are not built on this subject/answer principle.

The many episodes of the Adams cantos, however, are each built on the subject-rhyme or subject/answer principle, unlike episodes in musical fugue. The middle section of each Adams canto is built of strings of episodes that take flight around theme and counter-subject. Each of these episodes is organized on the basis of the juxtaposition of similar ideas spoken by two voices. For example, in Canto 63 we will find an episode on the ephemeral and the permanent. First the voice of Charles Francis Adams speaks of his grandfather's preference for serious literature over Scott's ephemeral fictions and of his grandfather's preference for land over less permanent forms of property. Then the voice of John Quincy Adams answers with a similar idea, the superiority of virtue over the ephemeral dreams of fancy. This episode, in turn, is part of a series of three episodes which move around the counter-subject topic of "change." While there is no syllogistic development of idea, there is a progressive illumination of the central idea as we move through the series of three episodes.

In other words, Pound exploits the subject-rhyme in each episode but also organizes the episodes in relation to each other so that he can exploit a sense of intellectual motion and interest.

Inversion can also be used to increase interest. Inversion is the turning of music upside down. Here again is the episode from Bach that we just looked at:

This is the pattern approximately, of the bass:

Bach inverted this pattern in the next episode, so that the soprano there is the same pattern as that of the first episode's bass, but upside down:

In Canto 63 Pound describes Benjamin Franklin, in one episode, as unpatriotic and selfish, and then in a later episode he turns the idea of the early episode on its head by describing Franklin as an unselfish citizen. This could as easily be called "reversal," of course; but we will see that Yeats, in transmitting his conversation with Pound about fugue, refers to the reversal of A B C D into D C B A as "inversion," and we may assume that Pound, thinking of fugal "inversion," spoke of it in that way.

Pound uses *stretto*, also, in Canto 63. Stretto is the overlapping of voices, so that the subject is not quite complete when the answer begins. The effect is of hurry and excitement, and perhaps of confusion. If stretto continues, constantly increasing the extent of the overlapping, the excitement and confusion increase. In music this effect depends, of course, on simultaneity.

To gain the same effect, Pound has his voices interrupt each other. He places his stretto just before the end of the fugue, a position often held by stretto in musical fugue, so that excitement builds and is then replaced by calm.

Finally, the "process" quality of fugue should be emphasized. In *Grove's Dictionary of Music* there is the suggestion that we should speak of music as written "in fugue" instead of saying that it is "a fugue." Fugue is not a sonnet-like form. In Pound's words, the "basic principle of counterpoint, as distinct from any set of niggling 'rules,' is that a number of melodic lines carry on and, by carrying on, interact" [*Music*, p. 459]. He stressed that composition is not by law [*GK*, p. 29], and he equated "process" and fugue in his discussion of the artist's shortcomings:

> You can cover it up more or less in symphonic or "harmonic" writing, you may even be able to camouflage it a little, a very much lesser little in counterpoint by patience and application of process. But you can't damn well learn even that process without learning a great deal by the way.
>   A fugue a week for a year wd. teach even a bullhead something. [*GK*, p. 114].

On the other hand, Pound recognized that the artist must control the strands so that the interaction would work. He was particularly impressed by Bach's "magnificent" structuring and control of the strands of polyphonic music. "Bach obviously could hear his own polyphony, the various lines going on all at once. . . . he had a direct perception of the added interest that came into music when two or more melodic lines interact" [*GK*, p. 153; *Music*, pp. 380, 403]. While this "added interest" may not be what we think of in the story line of a suspense novel, it should be kept in mind when we think of the form of fugue, and the analogy between fugue and *The Cantos*.

As we will see, Pound gains "added interest" from the interaction of voices in their linear motion through the poem, from the flight of episodes around the theme, and from the motion implicit in inversion's re-evaluation of an idea. He then adds stretto's increasing interest and excitement as he nears the end of the canto, so that we see an organization that is neither a rigid form nor a random repetition, but a process like fugue's patterning of patterns.

When Pound spoke of the analogy between *Cantos* and fugue he usually mentioned three ideas. One was this understanding that fugue is a process rather than a strict structure. Another is similar, the idea that the analogy between *Cantos* and fugue should not, itself, be thought of as a strict, one-to-one analogy. And the third is the focus on the comparison between the theme/response/counter-subject elements in fugue and the Nekuia/repeat/metamorphosis elements in *The Cantos*. We see these ideas in the first statement we have by Pound on the analogy between fugue and *The Cantos*, from the previously cited opening paragraph of his 1927 letter to his father:

> Dear Dad:-/-/Afraid the whole damn poem is rather obscure, especially in fragments. Have I ever given you outline of main scheme:::or whatever it is?
> I. Rather like, or unlike subject and response and counter subject in fugue.
> A.A. Live man goes down into world of Dead
> C.B. The "repeat in history"
> B.C. The "magic moment" or moment of metamorphosis, bust thru from quotidien [sic] into "divine or permanent world." Gods, etc. [*L*, p. 210].

First we notice that Pound does not say "structure," or "outline," or even "form." He speaks of the "main scheme," which is one way to describe the kind of patterning that fugue does.

Also, he doesn't say that *The Cantos* are like a fugue. He says that they are "rather like, or unlike subject and response and counter-subject in fugue."

Finally, we notice here, as we will each time Pound speaks of the way in which *The Cantos* resemble fugue, that he compares the opening themes of his poem to the subject/answer/counter-subject organization of fugue. If we think of Odysseus' descent into the past for knowledge in Canto 1 as a subject or theme, Pound's own descent into the past for knowledge in that canto is the repeat in history and the response to the opening subject (or theme) in fugue. Canto 2, then, the metamorphosis canto, counters Canto 1 in voice, in emphasis on the gods, and in its brilliant light imagery.

Pound probably described this analogy to Yeats much as he described it to his father, at about the same time and in some of the same words although in somewhat more detail. Yeats published the conversation in *A Packet for Ezra Pound* in 1929, and later as part of the introductory material to *A Vision*. The entire section on fugue from *A Packet* is quoted here:

> I shall not lack conversation. Ezra Pound, whose art is the opposite of mine, whose criticism commends what I most condemn, a man with whom I should quarrel more than with anyone else if we were not united by affection, has for years lived

in rooms opening on to a flat roof by the sea. For the last hour
we have sat upon the roof which is also a garden, discussing that
immense poem of which but seven and twenty Cantos are already
published. I have often found there some scene of distinguished
beauty but have never discovered why all the suits could not
be dealt out in some quite different order. Now at last he explains that it will, when the hundreth [sic] Canto is finished,
display a structure like that of a Bach Fugue. There will be no
plot, no chronicle of events, no logic of discourse, but two
themes, the descent into Hades from Homer, a metamorphosis from Ovid, and mixed with these mediaeval or modern historical characters. He has tried to produce that picture Porteous commended to Nicholas Poussin in 'Le Chef d'oeuvre
Inconnu' where everything rounds or thrusts itself without
edges, without contours—conventions of the intellect—form a
splash of tints and shades to achieve a work as characteristic
of the art* of our time as the paintings of Cezanne, avowedly
suggested by Porteous, as 'Ulysses' and its dream association
of words and images, a poem in which there is nothing that
can be taken out and reasoned over, nothing that is not a part
of the poem itself. He has scribbled on the back of an envelope
certain sets of letters that represent emotions or archetypal
events—I cannot find any adequate definition—A B C D and
then J K L M, and then each set of letters repeated, and then
A B C D inverted and this repeated, and then a new element
X Y Z, then certain letters that never recur and then all sorts
of combinations of X Y Z and J K L M and A B C D and D
C B A and all set whirling together. He has shown me upon the
wall a photograph of a Cosimo Tura decoration in three compart-
ments, in the upper the Triumph of Love and the Triumph
of Chastity, in the middle Zodiacal signs, and in the lower certain events in Cosimo Tura's day. The descent and the metamorphosis—A B C D and J K L M—his fixed elements, took the place
of the Zodiac, the archetypal person—X Y Z—that of the Triumphs, and certain modern events—his letters that do not recur—
that of those events in Cosimo Tura's day.
I may, now that I have recovered leisure, find that the mathematical structure, when taken up into imagination, is more
than mathematical, that seemingly irrelevant details fit together
into a single theme, that here is no botch of tone and colour—
Hodos Chameliontos—except for some odd corner where one
discovers beautiful detail like that finely modelled foot in Porteous' disastrous picture. It is almost impossible to understand
the art of a generation younger than one's own. I was wrong
about 'Ulysses' when I had read but some first fragments,
and I do not want to be wrong again—above all in judging verse.
Perhaps when the sudden Italian spring has come I may have
discovered what will seem all the more, because the opposite
of all I have attempted, unique and unforgetable [sic].

*Yeats' footnote: "Mr. Wyndham Lewis, whose criticism
sounds true to a man of my generation attacks this art
in 'Time and the Western Man'. If we reject, he argues, the

forms and categories of the intellect there is nothing left
but sensation, 'eternal flux'. Yet all such rejections stop
at the conscious mind, for as Dean Swift says in a medita-
tion on a woman who paints a dying face,

'Matter as wise logicians say
Cannot without a form subsist;
And form, say I as well as they,
Must fail, if matter brings no grist'."
[Yeats, *Packet*, pp. 1-4]

Here Yeats understands and describes the idea that the themes
move through the poem,–that the themes and not the sounds
of the poem are analogous to fugue. He mentions "inversion,"
and his "all sorts of combinations . . . set whirling together"
might well refer to stretto.

However, he describes the form as "like a Bach fugue,"
and does not transmit Pound's qualification, the suggestion
that the analogy is not to be understood as a strict enforcement
of a rigid form upon the poem. Yeats implies that fugue must be
the strong form that will rescue the poem from its present confusing state. This idea that *The Cantos* lack a strong form was
repeated by Yeats in his introduction to the *Oxford Book of
Modern Verse* in 1936, where he added a definition: "form must
be full, sphere-like, single" [Yeats, *Oxford*, p. xxv]. As we know,
fugue is not that.

Yeats' paragraph in *A Packet* may have been written as a defense of *The Cantos* against criticism by Wyndham Lewis. However, it could have had the reverse effect. Critics who found
The Cantos confusing and formless could have been influenced
by Yeats' belief that the poem needed a strong structure.

For example, Dudley Fitts, perhaps with Yeats' description
in mind, defended *A Draft of XXX Cantos* in 1930 on the ground
that the poem was contrapuntal. However, he had studied Pound's
early music criticism which stressed the sounds of counterpoint,
and he assumed that the structure was primarily "melodic and
rhythmic. . . . What Mr. Pound calls 'echo-counterpoint' is man-
aged in various ways; the most obvious device is that of repetition of pitch and rhythm . . ." Fitts missed the analogy between
theme and fugue, and, although his article in *Hound and Horn*
begins as a defense, it concludes with the belief that the poem
is only a "great attempt" [pp. 278-9].

On the other hand, Louis Zukofsky, to whom Pound had
explained the analogy to fugue, wrote a perceptive review for
The Criterion in the same year. He did not describe the analogy
between fugue and *Cantos*, but did suggest that the "loci" of
the poem move through it like the themes of polyphonic music.

"These three loci in Pound's world—they are present as hate, comprehension and worship, rather than as religious geometry—are often, next to each other or even continually intersecting . . ." [p. 429; see also *L*, p. 294]. This description is like Pound's own description of counter-point as lines that "carry on and, by carrying on, interact."

Zukofsky's careful and perceptive article did not impress the critics of the '30s. F.R. Leavis, for example, dismissed it as not seeming "to mean very much." Leavis, in fact, not only found the poem formless but discovered no content in it either. Instead, he praised *Mauberley* for both subject and form [Leavis, "Ezra," pp. 26-40].

In a letter to Hubert Creekmore in 1939 Pound wrote: "God damn Yeats' bloody paragraph. Done more to prevent people reading Cantos for what is *on the page* than any other one smoke screen" [*L*, p. 321]. However, Pound did not deny that there was an analogy between fugue and *The Cantos*, only that Yeats had not advanced the analogy helpfully.

Pound did not think Yeats knew what a fugue was:

> Well, I thought that he'd caused a good deal of confusion by talking about a "fugue," and as he wouldn't have known the difference between a fugue and . . . what shall we say? . . . I mean to say, his idea of fugue was very vague so he can't have known what the hell I was talking about. . . . I don't think Yeats knew what a fugue was . . . [EP/B, p. 172].

And in a letter to John Lackay Brown in 1937 about Yeats, and about Fitts, whose review had appeared in R.P. Blackmur's *Hound and Horn*, Pound said, "You are very right that Blackmur et sim. do *not*, etc. If Yeats knew a fugue from a frog, he might have transmitted what I told him in some way that would have helped rather than obfuscated *his* readers. Mah!!!" [*L*, p. 293]

But Pound continued to insist on the analogy itself. In this same letter to Brown he described the analogy to fugue in much the same way he had described it to his father ten years before:

> Take a fugue: theme, response, contrasujet. *Not* that I mean to make an exact analogy of structure.
>
> Vide, incidentally, Zukofsky's experiment, possibly suggested by my having stated the Cantos are in a way fugal. There *is* at start, descent to the shades, metamorphoses, parallel (Vidal-Actaeon). [*L*, p. 294]

Here again we have the parallel between theme in the poem and the subject/response/counter-subject in fugue, as well as the caution that this is not "an exact analogy."

Then, perhaps five years later yet, we have a similar example of Pound describing the poem in terms of fugure. Mary de Rachewiltz mentions in *Ezra Pound Father and Teacher* a conversation with Pound during the war. She quotes him as saying then:

> You know how a fugue of Bach is composed, one instrument comes in and the others repeat the theme. The Cantos start with Homer, the descent into hell. Then a theme of Ovid—Dafne, my own myth, not changed into a laurel but into coral. And then Dante—Dante has said everything there is to be said, so I start with Malatesta . . . [Rachewiltz, *Disc.*, p. 259]

Except for this conversation between Pound and his daughter, neither the 1940s nor the 1950s seem to provide any further statement on fugue and *The Cantos*. However, the 1960s and 1970s did produce many books and articles on the structure of *The Cantos*, and most of these mention the possibility of fugue as analogy for the poem's structure. In almost all cases this possiblity is not explained, and is dismissed as inaccurate, or inadequate, or inappropriate. One book, Daniel D. Pearlman's *The Barb of Time*, does explain how the analogy might work (pp. 11-19); and Hugh Kenner, at the close of his chapter on music in *The Pound Era* points out the similarity between subject-rhyme and polyphony. However, most criticism of this period does not take the analogy seriously. [but see Espey, pp. 75-77]

In fact, Stephen Adams, in his "Are *The Cantos* a Fugue?" discourages any attempt to pursue the analogy between fugue and *The Cantos*. He argues that it would be wrong to think of *The Cantos* as a fugue since poetry can never attain music's simultaneity. He recognizes Pound's "process" view of fugue, and the similarity between fugal structuring and Pound's poetic of juxtaposition, but argues that such musical procedures as inversion "correspond to nothing that can happen in language," and that further consideration of the analogy "must prove futile" [pp. 71, 74].

However, two critical statements written in 1977 use fugue as analogy for the structure of *The Cantos*. William McNaughton's "A Note on Main Form in *The Cantos*" describes the structure of the poem as three large fugues, corresponding to Inferno, Purgatorio, and Paradisio. He points to certain decads as subject, counter-subject, and stretto within each of these larger sections [*Pai*, 6, pp. 147-52]. The other statement, R. Murray Schafer's "Introduction" to his *Pound and Music*, repeats the belief which he first stated sixteen years before, that *The Cantos* remind him of fugue. He commends Pound for recognizing that the subject in fugue is an idea, not just a sound, and he points to the process aspect of fugue, regenerating "itself constantly from its own motivic material." He insists that there is an analogy between *The Cantos* and fugue, although this may be "discouraging for the critic who wants to see a structure he can draw on the blackboard" [*Music*, pp. 17-22] .

Let us now examine the fugue structuring in one canto, knowing that this pattern is not the rigid form Yeats hoped to find, but recognizing that the pattern speaks to us in an important way, adding a dimension to the poem that should be perceived.

"Voice" is of first importance to fugue and to Pound's use of fugue in the Adams cantos. The theme/response/counter-subject, as we recall from the Bach example earlier, are delivered by separate voices that move their separate, linear ways and interact. The theme/response/counter-subject, and the episodes and stretto in each Adams canto are also delivered by distinct voices that move through the poem separately, "and by carrying on, interact."

Canto 19 was written about the time Pound described his poem to his father and to Yeats as like fugue. It seems to me that he was working toward fugue in Canto 19 but that his control over the voices then was unsatisfactory, as I explained in Chapter Four. In the Adams cantos, however, I find a subtle and interesting interplay of voices, suggesting events in history and personalities of historical figures about whom I have some knowledge and respect. I enjoy the sound of John Adams' positive, stubborn voice, "No books, no time, no friends," set against his grandson's more ornate style, "deficiency in early moral foundations," or Cavalcante's voice, "in quella parte/dove sta memoria" set against Pound's "one up to Franklin." At the same time, the basic Eleusinian theme of *The Cantos* is maintained throughout the Adams cantos; Adams strives for enlightenment, and is the character Pound chose as the link between Purgatory and Paradise, dromena and epopte.

In writing the Adams cantos Pound drew excerpts from the *Works of John Adams* so that many voices are heard. In Canto 63 we hear Jeremiah Gridley, Fisher Ames, Charles Holt, Charles Francis Adams, John Quincy Adams, the young John Adams of the *Diary*, the mature John Adams of the *Autobiography*, the very old John Adams of the "Second Autobiography." We will also hear Cavalcante, and the people of Massachusetts, as well as at least two voices of the poet,—the fairly formal "ego scriptor cantilenae" and the less formal EP, who says "ditched" for dismissed. Once the voices are identified as separate, and can be heard entering the canto, conversing and agreeing with each other, the analogy to fugue is clear.

I have examined the entire canto here, dividing it voice by voice so that each quotation is spoken by a single voice. I identify each such subject by its source in the *Works of John Adams* and by its position in the pattern of the fugue. I have italicized the words and phrases Pound copied exactly from the source; partial underlining means that the form of the word was changed (as in *read*ing for read), and uninterrupted underlining means that entire phrases or sentences were taken from the original.

The pattern of fugue expressed in Canto 63 is:

> Opening subject/answer
>   First counter-subject/answer
>   Episodes suggested by first counter-subject
>   Episode suggested by opening subject
>   Second counter-subject/answer
>   Episodes suggested by second counter-subject
>   Stretto
>   Episode suggested by opening subject
> Final voice repeating the opening subject.

These divisions (and a section on "Fugue in the Adams Decad") will be used as captions in the discussion of the fugue and Canto 63.

Opening Subject/Answer: The subject or theme of Canto 63 is the idea that morality is necessary to government. Conflict results from the lack of morality. This opening subject will never be completely lost, throughout the canto, because all episodes are grounded on it even though they illustrate other ideas more explicitly.

The opening voice of the canto, Charles Francis Adams, describes the conflict between Hamilton and John Adams, and presents the theme. Hamilton, according to Charles Francis Adams, believed honor was a social rather than a moral condition, a belief that would lead to the duel with Burr and which, meanwhile, led him to take offense when Adams acted without his advice. This conflict between Hamilton and Adams is defined in terms of morality and deficiency of morality in government (I, 582-589):

> Towards sending of *Ellsworth*
> and the *pardon of Fries*
> *25 years in* office, treaties put thru and loans raised
> and *General Pinckney*, a man of honour
> declined to participate

or even to give *suspicion* of having colluded
deficiency in early moral foundations (Mr Hamilton's)
they *effect here and there* [63/351]

This might be paraphrased as follows: After twenty-five years in the service of his country, in office and in working for loans and making treaties, John Adams was attacked by Hamilton because he pardoned Fries and appointed Ellsworth without asking advice; General Pinckney, a man of honor, might have profited by this conflict but declined to participate in the attack; Hamilton's own moral deficiency caused this conflict.

The response, or answer, to this opening theme is given in the voice of President John Adams, addressing Congress at the time of the dedication of the city of Washington. He prays that George Washington's simple manners and true religion will flourish here, in the center of government named in honor of the first president [I, 592]:

simple manners
true religion, morals, here flourish
i.e. *Washington* [63/351]

Thus the subject which opened the canto, conflict caused by the lack of morality in government, is answered here in a different key, a prayer that the morality necessary for good government will be found at the nation's capital. The first voice, Charles Francis Adams, is answered by the second, President John Adams. This subject and answer will be echoed often and finally restated by the concluding voice speaking of the conflict between the English government and the colonies, caused by immoral law.

First Counter-Subject/Answer: The first counter-subject is the theme of change and it is introduced by the first voice, Charles Francis Adams. This is also in subject-rhyme, with the voice of Fisher Ames giving the answer. The counter-subject is [I, 602-607]:

4th March 1801
toward the newly created fount of supply (Mr Jefferson)
in ardour of hostility to Mr Jefferson
to overlook a good deed [63/351]

There are three changes identified here. The date refers to the inauguration of Jefferson and the change of government that it signified; the next line refers to the sudden diminution in John Adams' correspondence as requests were directed to the new president; and the last two lines refer to the change within the Federalist party as opposition to Jefferson began to unite the previously opposed factions. The canto reads "a good deed" for the text's "a great deal." It is possible that "a good deed" refers to John Adams' service to his country, and that irony is intended, but see Sanders [526-528] for a list of deviations from the text, including Canto 63's "hoarse laugh" for "horse laugh," and, "Thatcher," or "Thayer" for "Thacher."

The theme of change is answered in the voice of Fisher Ames who discussed change within the Federalist party in the first volume of the *Works of Fisher Ames*, quoted in a footnote in the *Works of John Adams* [I, 607n] :

> *If Pickering* cd/ mount on
> wd/ *vote for J. Adams* [63/351]

The Federalists, who had been unwilling to unite in support of John Adams in 1800, did unite sufficiently in opposition to Jefferson to support John Quincy Adams, together with Colonel Pickering, an Adams foe. Pound has identified father with son here, changing Ames' "vote for J. Q. Adams" to "vote for J. Adams."

Episodes Suggested by First Counter-Subject: This first counter-subject, "change." leads to three episodes. Each of these is a subject-rhyme and comments in some way on change while echoing the original subject's concern with morality, honor, or conflict.

The first episode suggests the changed public climate, as the country begins to honor John Adams in his old age. The first voice in this episode is that of Charles Francis Adams [I, 622] :

> *whose integrity not his enemies* had *disputed* [63/351]

and it echoes the conflict and concern with morality of the opening theme, at the same time suggesting that the public now found more to praise in John Adams than integrity.

The subject-rhyme, or answer, in this episode is a speech made to Adams at the time of the second constitutional convention of the Commonwealth of Massachusetts. Although spoken by one man, it might be said to be the voice of the public (I, 625] :

> *...rights*
> *diffusing knowledge of principles*
> *maintaining justice, in* registering *treaty of peace* [63/351]

Thus the episode, in speaking of the honors received by the eighty-five-year-old Adams, notes the change from the earlier years when he was President.

The next episode, drawn from two letters John Adams received at the time his son was elected President, also comments on both change and honor. The subject is given by Charles Holt, who had been prosecuted under the Alien and Sedition laws for his opposition to Adams. The letter congratulates Adams on the election of John Quincy Adams [I, 632] :

> *changed with the times, and not*
> forgetting what had suffered
> by *the sedition laws*
> *Obt. svt. Ch*as *Holt* [63/351]

and this is answered in the voice of John Quincy Adams who wrote his father as soon as he heard he had been elected (I, 632] :

> *Honoured father*
> (signed *John Quincy Adams* (in full)
> *1825* (when elected) [63/351]

suggesting the previous episode's theme of respect as well as commenting on the change of one President Adams into another.

The voice of Charles Francis Adams returns with the subject of the third episode, on the ephemeral and the permanent. He mentions his grandfather's willingness to listen to someone read anything to him, even Scott or Byron, although he preferred "more profound writers." He also notes that his grandfather's estate was almost entirely in land [I, 633] ;

> *Scott's fictions and even the vigorous* and *exaggerated*
> *poetry of* Ld/ *Byron*
> when they wd/ not read him anything else
> *property* EQUAL'D *land in* J. A.'s disposition [63/351]

contrasting the fictional and temporary with the permanent. The answer in this episode is in the voice of John Quincy Adams, a line from the epitaph he wrote for his parents' tomb [I, 643-4):

> *From Fancy's dreams to active Virtue turn* [63/351]

summing up the distinction between the ephemeral and the permanent and at the same time alluding to the previous theme of morality and, as we will see later, suggesting the theme of the second counter-subject, learning. With this line, too, the first counter-subject fades into the background of the canto; it will be echoed in Franklin's hypocrisy and implied in the second counter-subject, learning, but it is no longer in control of the canto.

Episode Suggested by Opening Subject: The next episode returns to the opening subject of the canto, the need for morality in government and the conflict that may result from immoral

government. Here the conflict is between Adams and Benjamin
Franklin at the time of the Revolution, when both were in Europe. The subject/answer shift in voice is not as clear in this episode as in the previous three, although it is not the stretto that
we will hear later in the canto. Instead, the voice of the subject
seems to be that of the old John Adams of the "Second Autobiography," assisted by the informal voice of the poet. So far
in this canto the poet's comments have been in the voice of
"ego scriptor cantilenae," a fairly objective if not formal voice,
but now the poet's voice is extremely informal, although not the
crackerbarrel of Canto 19 [I, 661-661]:

> The Cats *thought him* (Franklin) *almost a catholic*
> The Church of Engla*nd laid claim to *him as one of 'em*
> Presby*ters *thought him half presbyterian*
>   *friends, sec*taries,
> *Eripuit caelo fulmen* [63/351-352]

and the answer is in the informal voice of the poet, using a phrase
by John Adams [I, 663]:

> and all that to ditch *a poor man* fresh from the country [63/352]

so that the answer seems to sum up the conflict suggested by
the subject without an obvious subject/answer voice shift. The
phrase "a poor man" answers "Eripuit caelo fulmen" in the
following way: Adams believed that Franklin was hypocritical,
a man capable of controlling the media so as to seem to be the
friend of the poor,"pulling down the lightning from the sky" to
strike at tyranny, yet capable at the same time of subservience
to the French court. Thus, ironically, Franklin, the friend of the
poor, requested the dismissal of this "poor man" from America.
Furthermore, Adams believed that Franklin often seemed more
concerned for the welfare of the French government than for the
welfare of his own. This episode, then, returns to the opening
theme of conflict and immorality in government, with the conflict now between Adams and Franklin, rather than Adams and
Hamilton. Later in the canto we will see the episode "inverted"
with Franklin presented as an honest and concerned citizen.

Fugue in the Adams Decad: Before continuing with an examination of the second counter-subject of Canto 63, which is
introduced by the next line, let us look at that line, spoken by
the poet:

> Vol Two (as the protagonist saw it:) [63/352]

in terms of the Adams decad and *The Cantos* as a whole. Volume
One of the *Works of John Adams* is the life of John Adams from

the point of view of his grandson, Charles Francis Adams. It might be thought of as providing the subject or theme of the Adams decad, presented in Canto 62 and in the first part of Canto 63. Volume Two begins this same material, the life of John Adams, from the point of view of the protagonist, so that at this point in the decad we begin the answer, or response, to the decad's opening subject. Now we will hear the life of John Adams from the point of view of John Adams.

A counter-subject for the decad, drawn from Adams' political writings, will begin early in Canto 66 and will be answered from the point of view of Adams' state papers, beginning early in Canto 68. The final point of view in the decad, Adams' private correspondence, will begin the repetition of the opening subject of the decad.

If *The Cantos* as a whole are thought of as one fugue, the entire Adams decad can be thought of as the answer to the counter-subject stated in the Chinese cantos. William McNaughton, thinking of the poem as three fugues, has placed the Adams decad into the overall scheme as counter-subject in the second fugue. Either way of looking at the poem's organization makes sense, because of *The Cantos'* macrocosm-microcosm structure: thus, the episode's subject/answer is similar to the counter-subject's, which is similar in turn to the decad's, and that is similar in turn to a total fugue.

However the total poem is seen, though, this particular line half way through Canto 63 does clue us to a shift, not only of voice within the canto but of point of view within the decad, and the rest of the canto should be understood as forming part of the decad's answer to the opening subject, at the same time that it is heard as the second counter-subject, stretto, and final voice in the fugal construction of Canto 63.

The Second Counter-Subject/Answer: In Canto 63 the second counter-subject is closely linked to the first, since learning implies change, but it will be seen that the second half of the canto speaks about learning specifically, not about change in general. The counter-subject is introduced by "ego scriptor cantilenae" as a reference to the *Diary*,

> Vol Two (as the protagonist saw it:) [63/352]

In this volume John Adams describes what authors he read, what mistakes he made and how to avoid them in the future, what people to take as models and what character flaws to avoid, and, perhaps most important of all, how to use time wisely. He often returns to the question of whether it is better to study one book for a long period of time, or to alternate exercise and study, pleasure and work. This second counter-subject, learning, is answered in the voice of the young John Adams, the "protagonist" [II, 13-46]:

> *No books, no time, no friends*
> *Not* a *new idea* all *this week*
>   *even bagpipe not disagreeable*
> *for amusement read*ing her (*Mrs Savil*) the Ars Amandi
> 1758, around *half after* three, *went to the Court House*
> *With Sa*ml *Quincy and Dr* Gordon
> And *saw the most spacious room and*
>   *finest* line
> *of ladies* I *ever* did see, *Gridley*
> *enquired* my *method of study*
> and *gave me Reeve's advice to his nephew*
> read *a letter he wrote to Judge* Leighton: [63/352]

and this answer summarizes the main concerns of Volume Two: people, books, and time, especially as these are in turn concerned with learning.

Episodes Suggested by Second-Counter-Subject: The next seven episodes, suggested by this counter-subject, speak of study and profit, beginning, defining, reading, the use of time, memory, and character. Although earlier themes, such as honor, conflict and change, are often echoed or assumed, each of these episodes is primarily concerned with learning. They progress from the decision to study for the law to a study of character. Like the episodes suggested by the first counter-subject, these are each in subject/answer form.

The first episode, on study as opposed to profit, recalls the earlier theme of conflict. Jeremiah Gridley's voice gives the subject [II, 46]:

>   follow *the study*
> *rather than gain of the law*, but *the gain*
> *enough to keep out of the briars,* [63/352]

This advice occurs in one of the direct quotations within the text of Volume Two. It is answered by the voice of John Adams, taken from a footnote that quotes part of the *Autobiography* [II, 46n]:

> *So that I*
> *believe no lawyer ever did so much business*
> *for so little profit as I* during *the 17 years that I* practised
>   [63/352]

The voice of Gridley returns then with the subject of the next episode, how to begin the study of law [II,47]:

> *you must conquer the INSTITUTES*
> and *I began with Coke* upon *Littleton*
> > *greek mere matter* of *curiosity* (in the law)
> > > [63/352]

answered by the young John Adams [II, 47] :

> *to ask Mr. Thatcher's concurrence*
> *whole evening on original sin* and *the*
> > *plan of the universe*
> *and lastly on law,* he *thinks* that the country *is full* [63/352]

a summary of one of the first steps he took toward the study of law, an evening at Thacher's. At the beginning of the evening, two "beginnings" were discussed, original sin and the plan of the universe.

Perhaps the difficulty in defining these terms suggested the next episode, on definition. In discussing books, a page later in the *Diary* John Adams notes the need for definition: "this is the first thing a student ought to aim at, namely, distinct ideas under the terms, . . ." and here he refers to books that define [II, 48] :

> *Van Myden editio terza design of* the *book is*
> exposition

> of *technical terms*
> as *of Hawkins' Pleas of the Crown.* [63/352-353]

and a visual sense of simultaneity is **gained** by seeing the ideogram for Cheng, "true," [See *Comp, 63*: pp. 37, 38, concern for terminology] in the center of Adams' statement, so that in this episode subject and answer can be heard simultaneously.

The next episode moves away from beginnings to the work and study of the next years. John Adams of the *Autobiography* gives the subject [II, 50] :

> > > *Bracton,*
> *Britten, Fleta* on *Glanville,* [63-353]

a list of books that he had at that time, in a comment on his need for a good library, which he eventually acquired. The young John Adams answers with a description of his studies during those years [II, 52-53] :

> > > must *dig with my fingers*
> as *nobody will lend me or sell me a pick axe.*

Exercises my lungs, revives *my spirits opens my pores*
read*ing Tully* on *Cataline quickens* my *circulation* [63/353]

This same voice, from the *Diary* several pages later, introduces the subject of Ruggles' character in an episode that echoes the early subject of morality and suggests the later concern with time, and how to spend that wisely [II, 67]:

*Ruggles grandeur in boldness of thou*ght *honour contempt*
of meanness
[63/353]

The answer is by Charles Francis Adams from a footnote [II, 67n]:

was practising law and running *a tavern in Sandwich*
*died Novascotia 1*788 and a tory. [63/353]

an introduction to John Adams' own multiple use of time and to his stubbornness, too, perhaps.

Throughout this part of the *Diary* the young John Adams is worried about how to learn, how to "wear" something "into his mind" and "learn easier and sooner" [p. 68]. He did not spend a whole day on one book, but indulged instead in what he thought was a "wavering life" [II, 69]:

Read one book an *hour*
then dine, smoke, cut wood [63/353]

and this concern with how to learn is answered in the voice of Cavalcante:

in quella parte
dove sta memora, [63/353]

"in that part where the memory is," (*Index,* p. 100).

An inversion of the earlier episode on Franklin is contained in the next episode, on character. Earlier, the voice of the eighty-year-old John Adams described Franklin as more interested in France's welfare than in that of his own country. Here, in the second half of an episode on character, the young John Adams will describe Franklin as a concerned citizen. The subject of the episode is the character of Colonel Chandler, to whom study has not brought dignity [II, 74-75]:

Colonel Chandler not conscious
these crude thoughts and expressions
are catched up *and treasured as proof of his character.* [63/353]

This subject is answered in the same voice with an inversion of the earlier episode on Franklin: the elder Adams of the "Second Autobiography" saw Franklin as immoral and hypocritical; the young Adams of the *Diary* praises his character [II, 81]:

> *Not find*ing them (Rhine Grapes *slips*) *in* that *city*
> *sends to a village 70 miles away*
>   *and then sends* two packets
> *one by water and lest* that *miscarry, the other by* post
> *to Mr* Quincey *to whom he owes nothing*
>   *and with whom* he is *but little acquainted*
>   *purely for the* purpose of
> *propagating* Rhine wine in *these provinces* [63/353]

suggesting Franklin's scholarly interests as well as his courtesy
and carefulness.

Stretto: A stretto, the rapid interchange by "ego scriptor
cantilenae," EP, the young John Adams, and Cavalcante, brings
the counter-subject to a close and ties it to the conflict of the
opening subject. The informal voice of the poet opens the stretto
with a reference back to the previous episode, and at the same
time back to the first Franklin episode, which reflected the
opening subject:

> (one up to Franklin) [63/353]

and the young John Adams speaks of anger and the mind [II,
pp. 87-88]:

> I
> *read Timon of Athens, the manhater*
> *must be* [63/353]

and this comment, the original of which is "I find that the mind
must be agitated with some passion, either love, fear, hope,
&c., before she will do her best," is interrupted and clarified by
the poet speaking as "ego scriptor cantilenae:"

> (IRA must be) aroused ere [63/353]

Then the young Adams finishes his comment:

> *the mind* be
>   at its *best* [63/353]

and Cavalcante closes the stretto with

> *la qual manda fuoco* [63/353]

"which sends fire," [*Index*, p. 118].

If interest has increased throughout a fugue, it will peak at
a point just before the calm of the ending, and stretto with its
intensity often occurs at that penultimate moment. In every
Adams canto that contains stretto it occurs at that same point.
See *The Cantos of Ezra Pound*, p. 362, "these were the letters
. . . George IIIrd." or p. 378, "Nor where who sows . . . Mr Eliot
left us" or p. 401, "(meaning placing one) . . . Mr Blomberg is
ill."

In those cantos that do not contain stretto, an angry passage or tirade in the poet's voice may appear at this point. See p. 350, "Snot, Bott, Cott . . . the Prime snot." The vignette *in margine*," p. 407, does double duty as an intense passage analogous to stretto both for Canto 69 and for the Adams decad as a whole.

Episode Suggested by Opening Subject: This next episode brings the canto back to the opening theme and at the same time introduces the final voice of the canto. The subject of the episode, the conflict between morality and immorality in government, is introduced by the young John Adams, speaking of the misuse of law by the fraudulent and ambitious [II, 90-117]:

> *dirty and ridiculous litigations been multiplied*
> *proverb; as litigious as Braintree*
> *fraud and system of bigotry*
> *on which papal usurpations are founded, monument of priestly*
> *ambition*
> guile wrought into *system* [63/353]

answering it in the voice of "an old man, turned of seventy" which he assumes in order to write an anonymous letter to a newspaper. The draft of the letter is included in the *Diary* [pp. 120-123] and speaks of the irony of believing in English liberty when laws can be manipulated by those who scheme to do so [II, 121]:

> *'Our constitution' 'every man his own monarch'*
> *all these* boasting *speeches have heard* (1760)
> *and never failed to raise a* hoarse *laugh* [63/353-354]

so that the episode, with its subject and answer on fraudulent use of the law, brings the canto back to the opening theme.

Final Voice Repeating the Opening Subject: John Adams, speaking in the *Autobiography*, repeats the opening subject [II, 124-125n]:

> *An inferior officer in Salem*
> *whose name was Cockle petitioned*
> *the justices* for a *Writ of Assis*tance
> *to break open ships, shops, cellars* and *houses*
> *Mr Sewall expressed doubt of legality,*
> *Oxenbridge Thayer with Otis*
> *a contest appeared to be opened.* [63/254]

At the opening of the canto, Hamilton's "deficiency in early moral foundations" caused the conflict between Adams and Hamilton; here Cockle's immoral attempt to use the law to "break open ships, shops, cellars and houses" will lead to the Revolution.

Let us look back now at the pattern of the fugue in Canto 63. First, two voices agree that morality is necessary to government. The topic of change is then introduced, not as a result, or cause, or opposite, or negation, but as an idea that might shed "a cross-light" on morality and government. Three illustrations are then offered, so that we can use the idea of change to illuminate the idea of morality. A President's integrity, or morality, is for a while the only thing praised about him, and then public opinion changes so that some other practical virtues are commended; his son is elected president and his own past errors are forgiven; he preferred the permanent both in literature and in property, and, finally, virtue, the permanent and ideal morality, is contrasted to changing Fancy. We have taken a short flight around the central theme (morality) in terms of the counter-subject (change) and have come to rest again.

There is now a comment on Franklin's lack of morality in government, the negative half of an inversion. This episode rhymes with the opening subject as Franklin's immorality rhymes with Hamilton's, and it is possible now to move from negative to positive, a motion that reflects the shift from the counter-subject "change," to the more positive counter-subject, "learning."

With this second counter-subject we take flight again for a longer arc around the central theme. First we are introduced to learning, the decision to study in spite of the risk of not earning money; then the beginnings, and definitions; then the process of study itself, reading and the use of time and memory; finally the result in character, and we are back again at the central theme of morality. Here, too, is the second half of the inversion, giving us the positive view of Franklin.

Stretto, as I have mentioned, occurs here, close to the end of the canto so that it can intensify interest and pleasure. The canto moves faster, and with a melopoeic concord, "must be (IRA must be) aroused ere the mind be at its best/ la qual manda fuoco," that rests within the intense discord of interrupting voices.

We return to a final statement of the opening theme, which in this canto does not have fugue's sense of calm. Here there is a tone almost of doom as the future Revolution hovers over the final statement. We know that the conflict will result in better government, largely because of John Adams' integrity, but the canto ends in suspense, with the tension still unresolved. In fact, while the fugue of Canto 63 has come to a close, the larger fugue of the Adams canto is still in an early stage of its exposition, the response to the opening statement, and we are waiting here for the counter-subject. Thus, even as the flight of the smaller fugue comes to rest, the arc of the larger fugue's flight has just begun.

Fugue is not the only structuring device in the Adams cantos. There is ideogram, and the nesting of microcosm within macrocosm. In the next chapter I will describe the Schifanoia Frescoes, mentioned by Yeats in *A Packet*, examining that analogy as a structuring force in one of the Pisan cantos, but fresco is at work in the Adams cantos also; Zeus presides over the entire decad, and I think Proteus may preside over Canto 63, a poem defining change, revolution, and learning.

Plate 2. Month of March.

Plate 1 :

Plate 3: Month of April.

CHAPTER SIX

FRESCO

> . . . the Schifanoia, that
> might give a clue . . .

Yeats, in the explanation of fugue which we examined in the last chapter, also mentioned the Schifanoia Frescoes:

> He has shown me upon the wall a photograph of a Cosimo Tura decoration in three compartments, in the upper the Triumph of Love and the Triumph of Chastity, in the middle Zodiacal signs, and in the lower certain events in Cosimo Tura's day. The descent and the metamorphosis—A B C D and J K L M—his fixed elements, took the place of the Zodiac, the archetypal persons—X Y Z—that of the Triumphs, and certain modern events—his letters that do not recur—that of those events in Cosimo Tura's day. [Yeats, *Packet*, p. 3]

And Pound, in the Bridson interview from tapes made in 1959 when the poem neared completion, endorsed that part of Yeats' description:

> . . . the Schifanoia Frescoes I discovered after I had done something similar. The Schifanoia does give—there is an analogy there. That is to say, you've got the contemporary life, you've got the seasons, you've got the Zodiac and you have the Triumphs of Petrarch in different belts—I mean, that's the only sort of map or suggestion of a map. No, the Schifanoia, that might give a clue . . . [EP/B, p. 172]

Beginning with an examination of the Schifanoia Frescoes themselves, then of their similarity to Canto 81, and finally of their similarity to *The Cantos* as a whole, this chapter will describe how fresco works as analogy for structuring in *The Cantos*.

The Schifanoia Frescoes or "months" were twelve paintings, each focused on a classical god or event and each divided into subsets or clusters of scenes. They were painted on the walls of the Salone dei Mesi or Room of the Months [See Plate 1] in the Schifanoia Palace in Ferrara, Italy, a palace built, or rebuilt so extensively as to be a new building, by Borso d'Este during the 1460s. The room is about twenty-five yards long, twelve wide and eight high. There were originally twelve panels, four on the north wall, three on the two side walls and two on the south, but the palace was neglected during the centuries that followed its construction. The Frescoes were concealed under a coat of whitewash and some were destroyed while the room was used as a tobacco factory, warehouse, and tannery. The seven remaining Frescoes were rediscovered in the early 19th Century and have since been renovated. In Plate 1 we cannot see March, but the Frescoes from April through September (moving from right to left, counter-clockwise around the room) are visible. March and April [See Plates 2 and 3] probably in one photograph, were undoubtedly the Frescoes that Yeats wrote about, since April would be the triumph of love, March the triumph of chastity.

It is now assumed that Cosimo Tura, having planned the room, did not actually paint the Frescoes. [See D'Ancona for a history of the room.] At the time Pound wrote the early cantos, however, Tura was thought to have been the artist, and in Canto 24 Pound said of the room:

> Albert made me, Tura painted my wall,
> And Julia the Countess sold to a tannery . . . [24/114]

Later, other artists including Francesco del Cossa and Ercole Roberti were recognized as having painted some of the Frescoes, with del Cossa undoubtedly the artist of the March and April Months which Pound alluded to in his conversation with Yeats and also in the Pisan Cantos. He commented on the new attribution in Canto 79:

> Guard's cap quattrocento passes *a cavallo*
> on horseback thru landscape Cosimo Tura
> or, as some think, Del Cossa . . . [79/485]

The style of each Fresco, as well as its subject (dictated by season), differs slightly from the style and subject of any other, so that each Fresco has its own individuality. All, however, maintain a three-part form, with a divine scene at the top, an earthly scene at the bottom and a depiction of the zodiac at the center on a dark background. This center section, repeated in all Frescoes, creates a dark band around the room, dividing paradise from earth.

Because Pound spoke of his own paradise and purgatory, usually in terms of Dante's, it is tempting to assume that the three-part hell/purgatory/paradise form of the *Divine Comedy* is also present in the Frescoes. Notice that Yeats, however, in equating Pound's poem with the Frescoes, does not at any time mention a "hell." Although Pound thought of the poem as containing a hell, he also spoke of the three-part division as simply "the casual, the recurrent, and the permanent." And even though the poem contains moments of hate and avarice, the Schifanoia Frescoes do not; they contain earthly and divine scenes, the two divided by symbols of time.

In fact, the bottom section of a Fresco, far from being similar to any hell, is a presentation of paradise on earth, characterized by nature, the seasons, and the court of Borso d'Este in Ferrara. Look at the photograph of the Month of March (Plate 2). Like Pound's *Cantos*, the subjects in the bottom section are juxtaposed without narrative or syllogistic order. We see scenes of March, early Spring, especially those that illustrate themes proper to Minerva: wise, chaste, just, and proper people, actions and events. Borso at the right dispenses justice; Borso and his court leave for the hunt; on horseback Borso and his court appear again near the top of the section. This unfinished scene may have been one that Pound remembered at Pisa, "Guard's cap quattrocento passes *a cavallo/* on horseback thru landscape." These men could be wearing either U.S. Army fatigue caps or campaign caps. Also, just to the left of the men on horseback, we see the other scene recalled at Pisa:

> —niggers comin' over the obstacle fence
> as in the insets at the Schifanoja
> (del Cossa) to scale, 10,000 gibbet-iform posts supporting
> barbed wire [77/473]
>
> . . .
> and those negroes by the clothes-line are extraordinarily
> like the figures del Cossa
> Their green does not swear at the landscape [78/477]

Pound is comparing posts, clotheslines and soldiers to the grape arbor and the men there tying and trimming the vines. This occupation, proper to the season, will be echoed in a later Fresco; the lower section of September contains a scene of the grape harvest.

In the bottom section of the Month of April (Plate 3), events suggest moments appropriate to Venus, the goddess of April, and to that season in Ferrara. Borso and his men return from the hunt; Borso is surrounded by his courtiers; he watches the annual race to the Church of San Sebastian. The courtiers and their ladies watch the young men and girls race, and the ladies in the windows at the left look down on one of the

spectators as he glances up at them, an allusion to the flirtations that surround the upper section of the Fresco, as well as
to actual events, since the windows formed a natural gallery
around the square and were used as such here as well as in other
Italian Renaissance towns.

Each of the upper sections of the Frescoes contains a divine person on a car drawn by symbolic animals forward and
to the viewer's left (toward the next month), surrounded by
symbols in human or earthly form. Minerva, goddess of chastity
and wisdom, rides in a car drawn by two unicorns and is surrounded by jurists and weavers in the upper section of March;
and Venus, on a car drawn by two swans and surrounded by
lovers and rabbits (symbols of fertility) accepts the veneration
of the kneeling Mars. The three graces are at the upper right.
These are the scenes referred to by Pound as the Triumphs of
Petrarch. A triumph of victors was a Roman parade like those
in which states of saints are carried on floats or chariots now,
in Spain during Holy Week. Petrarch wrote twelve cantos which
describe six such triumphs, each a victor over the condition
which preceded it: love, chastity, death, fame, time, eternity.
Love, which begins by conquering lust, is described at his triumph:

> A leader, conquering and supreme, I saw,
> Such as triumphal chariots used to bear
> To glorious honor on the Capitol.
>   . . .
> Four steeds I saw, whiter than whitest snow,
> And on a fiery car a cruel youth
> With bow in hand and arrows at his side.
>   No fear had he, nor armor wore, nor shield,
> But on his shoulders he had two great wings [Petrarch, pp. 5-6]

a description that might apply to a Schifanoia Fresco such as
April, which seems to have conquered the March, since Mars
kneels before love.

The divine characters of the upper sections are in human
form (with the exception of the female cyclopes in September) and they are dressed in Ferrara's fashions. Mars, therefore,
suggests not only the subordination of war to love, March to
April, but the Renaissance courtier to his lady, an identification of the divine with earthly present that would appeal to the
poet who saw in Venetian black shawls a reverence for Demeter's
grief.

There is some use of perspective in the upper sections, as well as within the component scenic parts. Figures in the foreground are larger than the three graces, for example, and the scenes are balanced around the central god or goddess, so that while the upper and lower sections seem somewhat alike in theme and in their crowded scenes of stylish Renaissance figures, they differ in balance. The bottom sections seem more "casual," to use Pound's word.

The center sections are painted on an intense and dark blue ground. They contain no scenes, and the figures, zodiac symbols and decans out of Eastern mythology that preside over time, are neither scenically related like those in the upper sections nor juxtaposed and thematically related like those in the lower sections, although the Renaissance artists have given human and thematic attributes to these mythological creatures. In each Fresco there are three pictures evenly spaced along the plain ground. The center picture is of two figures, the lower of which is the zodiac symbol for the month. The upper center figure, and the two side pictures are of the decans, each of which presides over ten days [D'Ancona, pp. 11-12; Lindsay]. In March the sun rises in the zodiac sign of the ram, Aries. The first decan, at the left, is descended from the ancient Egyptian sacrificer, and is in accord with the theme of wisdom and justice. The center decan, presiding over the second ten-day period in the month, seems to float above the ram, and her ancient attributes (horses' hooves) are hidden beneath her Renaissance dress. The final decan holds an arrow and ring. In the Month of April the sun rises beneath the sign of the starred Taurus, the bull. The first decan, a mother and child, is not clearly related to astrology but is closely related to the April theme. The other two decans are more obvious echoes of the older symbolism. At the center, above the bull, the second decan holds a key, and the third (*homo ferus*, descended from the boar and still with boar's fangs) holds a snake/dragon and an arrow, attributes of earlier symbols [D'Ancona, pp. 36-37].

The names of the decans vary; one list contains *Eros* and *Satan*, but not all do. Also, the shapes vary. Although most were originally beasts, such as crocodile or snake, others were part human. In the Schifanoia Frescoes there are few obvious indications of the original beasts, demi-gods, or emblems. Although the third decan of April has fangs and the third decan of June has clawed feet, most have been humanized. They seem distant, however, when we comapre them to the very human,

High Renaissance figures in the other sections. These zodiac figures represent time, not people, and they symbolize the condition people must cope with, or in Pound's phrase, the condition that must be "got thru" [82/523] to attain even momentary paradise. As such, the center band is analogous to the dromena's darkness and confusion. Because the dark band in the Room of the Months divides the divine world of the gods from the earthly world, this sense of dark dromena is most intense as the entire room is viewed.

Moving around the Room, through the Frescoes that remain, we may not at once see a clear "triumph" of one god or theme over the previous one, such as we saw in April's triumph over March's chastity. However, all of the Frescoes maintain their three-part form, their emphasis on a theme indicated by a central god or goddess, and their emphasis on cyclic time, the seasons and the Zodiac.

Apollo presides over May and the theme of that month is apparently poetry and the arts. Aurora guides Apollo's car; the nine muses are at his left; poets or scholars stroll at his right. The twins at the bottom right of the upper section repeat the zodiac symbol for the month, Gemini. Most of the bottom section has been lost. A door was cut through the wall there, destroying scenes of harvest, of Borso accepting a basket of cherries, of laborers pruning trees, of a donkey crossing a bridge.

In June we recognize the god, Mercury, by his attributes since the figure of the god himself has been lost. He has the lyre and caduceus and he is surrounded by scenes of trade and commerce. In the middle section the sun rises in the sign of cancer, and as in all center sections, decans flank and cap the zodiac sign.

Moving to the north wall of the Room we see the Fresco for July. Jupiter's car is drawn by lions. He shares his triumph with Cybele, goddess of earth, and they are surrounded by monks, the military, and a Ferrara wedding. As in all upper sections there is here, in spite of the centered god and a general sense of scenic balance, a practical as well as thematic affinity with the lower sections.

August is the Triumph of Ceres, and the first decan holds wheat and the pomegranate. At Ceres' right a farmer is plowing and sowing, and around the triumphal car we see merchants and bags of produce. Proserpine and Dis are at the upper right, and the zodiac symbol for the month is the virgin.

September ought to be the Triumph of Vulcan, but instead it is presided over by Lust, and we see Mars and Venus in bed at her left, with Vulcan's furnace and the female cyclops at her right. This is the least conventionally humanized of the upper sections. September is the time of the grape harvest and at the right of the bottom section the men are now harvesting the grapes from the arbor we first saw in the Month of March, at which time they were pruning and tying the vines. The zodiac symbol is Libra, the balance scale.

The Room of the Months is the result of these separate Frescoes. It surrounds the viewer with scenes of life on earth which reflect the permanent world of the gods and the recurrence of the seasons. One obvious similarity, then, between *The Cantos* and the Frescoes is the nesting structure of both. As we have seen in previous chapters, the poem is structured from subjects within cantos within larger sections, and the Salone dei Mesi is a work of art composed of separate Frescoes, and each Fresco is a work of art composed of three sections, each of which, in turn, is composed of separate scenes.

But there are other similarities in the structuring of poem and Frescoes. While some of these seem more obvious in the late cantos, most exist throughout the poem, a condition Pound alluded to when he said in 1959 that he "had done something similar" even before discovering the Frescoes. I think that this similarity rests primarily in Pound's veneration for and invocation of the gods, but before reviewing that element in the entire poem, let us look at the parallels between the Frescoes and the first two pages of Canto 81.

The bottom section in a Fresco is created, like Pound's poem, of subjects juxtaposed without obvious order, and it is fairly easy to see what Yeats meant in equating these scenes of fifteenth-century Ferrara with "certain modern events," or events that occurred during Pound's life. If we look at pages 517-18 for example, we see several scenes juxtaposed. All of them have ,to do with Iberian culture (Spain, Portugal, the Canaries), all are contemporary with Pound's life, and all seem, in their expression of vigorous life, to rhyme:

> forty years gone, they said: go back to the station to eat
> you can sleep here for a peseta"
> > goat bells tinkled all night
> > and the hostess grinned: Eso es luto, haw!
> mi marido es muerto
> > (it is mourning, my husband is dead)
> when she gave me paper to write on
> with a black border half an inch or more deep,

```
       say 5/8ths, of the locanda
   "We call all foreigners frenchies"
   and the egg broke in Cabranez' pocket,
            thus making history. Basil says
   they beat drums for three days
   till all the drumheads were busted
            (simple village fiesta)
   and as for his life in the Canaries. . .
   Possum observed that the local portagoose folk dance
   was danced by the same dancers in divers localities
            in political welcome. . . [81/517-8]
```

Eliot's description of the dance and Bunting's of the fiesta are
rhymes, and probably the event of the egg rhymes on Pound's
stay with the Spanish widow. All four seem to be lively, friendly
events, Chaucerian in their vitality, and we can easily associate
them with the bottom section. They are juxtaposed in a thematically reasonable but not syllogistically or narratively reasonable
way.

There are moments in Canto 81 that communicate something
analogous to the conditions expressed by the Frescoes' center
band, but these moments are not as readily identified as the
casual modern events of the bottom section were. Nevertheless,
they are there. The figures of the Schifanoia center sections
represent time itself, the condition through which one strives
for grace, or enlightenment, or a momentary glimpse of "Gods,
etc." In Canto 81 Pound says of his own life, "To break the pentameter, that was the first heave," an allusion to his struggle to
create *Cantos* out of "Urcantos," as well as his contribution
to the creation of the early twentieth-century poetic renaissance.
The pentameter thus represents the kind of time (both in verse
and in life), and the kind of darkness that must be overcome.
There are rhymes on this allusion to struggle, and one of them
specifically mentions the descent:

```
   Sargent had painted her
            before he descended
   (i.e. if he descended
            but in those days he did thumb sketches,
   impressions of the Velázquez in the Museo del Prado [81/517]
```

In 1887 Henry James wrote an article for *Harpers* about John
Singer Sargent in which he seemingly contradicted himself. He
began by saying that Sargent's style had not changed, but then
he discussed Sargent's earlier Spanish period, lasting only two
years, its Impressionism and failure in contrast to the later period.
While in Spain Sargent had painted "El Jaleo," a Spanish dancer
described by James as ugly and "wanting in serenity." He preferred

the very Jamesian "Lady with a Rose" of the post-Spanish period, and he suggested that if Sargent did change it was for the better, a move away from Impressionism and imitations of Velázquez toward painting in which the artist "sees deep into his subject, undergoes it, absorbs it, discovers in it new things that were not on the surface, becomes patient with it, and almost reverent, and, in short, enlarges and humanizes the technical problem" [James, p. 115]. Pound's statement in Canto 81 about Sargent is thus an allusion to an artist (James) who may or may not have found in another artist (Sargent) evidence of descent and metamorphosis. The scene is of Sargent's early Spanish period, and is thematically in accord with Pound's stay in Spain, Eliot's Portuguese dance, and Bunting's village festival, especially if Sargent's painting from this period of the dancer, "El Jaleo" is recalled. But the descent reference rhymes most forcefully with Pound's own struggle to create artistic metamorphosis, "to break the pentameter."

The opening lines of Canto 81 present a triumph analogous with an upper section in a Schifanoia Fresco:

> Zeus lies in Ceres' bosom
> Taishan is attended of loves
> under Cythera, before sunrise [81/517]

This image describes the camp at Pisa, as Hugh Kenner has shown in *The Pound Era*:

> North and east stretched moutains, one cone-shaped above deli-
> cate trees (he named it Taishan, for China's sacred peak), two to
> the left of it low and hemispherical (he named them the Breasts
> of Helen). Pisa lay south; peering through the dangling laundry
> on clear days one could see the Tower. Sun and moon rose over
> the mountains, set over the invisible sea. [Kenner, *Era*, p. 417].

At the same time, the scene is the Triumph of Aphrodite, centered at the top of Pound's canto, above Zeus and Demeter, so that love triumphs over power and earth. Cythera, her name as she is born out of the sea foam, suggests Botticelli's painting and recalls other allusions in *The Cantos*: "she like a great shell curved," [17/76] "O Queen Cytherea,/ che 'l terzo ciel movete," [91/617] and it is the means of identifying Aprhodite and Kuanon:

> in this air as of Kuanon
> enigma forgetting the times and seasons
> but this air brought her ashore a la marina
> with the great shell borne on the seawaves [74/443]

We can thus see Aphrodite/Kuanon as a clue to the theme of the Pisans and to Canto 81 with its village festivals and dances, as well as its awareness of artistic struggle. Or, to put it another way, the presence of the goddess above the other divinities marks the importance of love above power or wealth in animating both the dance and the struggle.

Since Pound said in 1959 that he "had done something similar" to the Schifanoia Frescoes, we might assume that the allusions to the gods beginning in Canto 1 may be taken as clues to themes governing cantos, much as the divinities in the Frescoes indicate themes for each month. When the separate cantos are examined in this way, with the Frescoes held in the mind, we often see in the references to specific divinities (or in seemingly offhand comments such as the "oh my Clio" of Canto 19) imagery that enlivens the themes. Pound emphasized this relationship between god and theme by opening several cantos with imagery of divinities. Consider the following opening lines:

> These fragments you have shelved (shored).
>   "Slut!" "Bitch!" Truth and Calliope
> Slanging each other sous les lauriers: [8/28]
>   . . .
> Compleynt, compleynt I hearde upon a day,
>   Artemis singing, Artemis, Artemis
>   Agaynst Pity lifted her wail: [30/147]
>   . . .
>
> and the wave concealed her,
>   dark mass of great water. [96/651]
>   . . .
> The boat of Ra-Set moves with the sun [98/684]
>   . . .
> Came Neptunus
>   his mind leaping
>   like dolphins, [116/695]

Furthermore, almost every canto either specifically mentions a presiding deity or implies one. The god may not be one of the great Olympians, but a lesser god such as Proteus or even a human parody of the god. For example in Canto 9 we learn that Sigismundo "built a temple" to Isotta, and later [76/459] we learn that she is divine, "Divae Ixottae." Gods presiding over the cantos of the "palette," the first eleven cantos, are Aphrodite [1/5], Neptune [2/9], Kore [3/11], Artemis [4/14], Hymen [5/17], Sirens [6/21], Eros [7/27], Truth and Callipe [8/28], Isotta [9/41], Sigismundo [10/46], Zeus [11/50]. The scenes are usually more complex than such a list suggests. Canto 2, like the Thrones decad, contains many gods, and if Neptune seems to preside it is because references to him enclose the references to Dionysus, Proteus and the fauns. Also, a reference can be ironic, as in Canto 10 where Pound appropriates Pope Pius the Second's satiric use of the crucifixion of Christ.

The gods mentioned in the first eleven cantos, even Malatesta with his striving toward the divine, are necessary pigments on the palette. Each will serve to unite future strands in the poem, Odyssean, sexual, paternal. At the same time each works to structure the immediate canto over which it presides. And, just as within each canto there is a presiding god, so within each of the larger sections of the poem there is one canto that rises above the other cantos in lyricism and in worship of the divine, so that each of these sections is presided over by a god's triumph, and the poem moves from an Eleusinian dromena ruled by Persephone [Canto 17] to a state of awareness presided over by Cavalcante's God of Love [Canto 36], to the fecundity surrounding Demeter [Canto 47], to the learning and order presided over by Zeus [71(256) and 421], to the paradise of Kuanon [Canto 74], back to a state of self-knowledge and learning at the altar of Artemis [Canto 91], through to a vision in Thrones of all the gods [Canto 106], and finally to a human earthly paradise. Like the Room of the Months, such a progress would not be narratively clear; scenes of contemporary life and the repeats in history might distract from or momentarily deny the divine themes.

These allusions to the gods are part of the Eleusinian pattern we first met in Chapter One, in the quotation from Pound's letter to his father. The poem is constantly aware of the "Gods, etc.," an awareness appropriate to an epic.

In the next chapter I will trace the ways in which all of the analogies may apply to one canto at once, but before moving to that summation I would like to return to the relationship of Fresco to these other analogies. It is, like all of them, an analogy to the structure of the poem rather than a structure governing the poem. It is a "suggestion of a map," not the original from which a poetic map is created. The similarity is between the structuring process that created the Frescoes (nesting, juxtaposition, thematic order, cyclic order) and the structuring process that created the poem. And, like ideogram but more imagistically specific, this structuring proceeds in the mind of the reader who groups ideas and images offered by the poem on the page. Although Canto 81 and a few other cantos open with an image of divine scene, there is no consistent ordering of the words on the page that corresponds with the consistent pattern of upper/middle/lower section within a Fresco. In this way the Fresco analogy differs importantly from the analogy to fugue, which is based on the subject rhymes as they appear in subject rhyme schemes on the page. We will see, in the next chapter, how these and other structuring devices occur simultaneously in Canto 116.

CONCLUSION

In previous chapters a term or analogy was first defined and then used more or less independently in an examination of the poem. Now, using four of the more complex analogies together (descent/repeat/metamorphosis, ideogram, fugue, and the Schifanoia Frescoes) we will study the structuring patterns of one canto.

Canto 116 is part of Pound's earthly paradise and it opens with a moment of metamorphosis, a glimpse of the divine world of the gods, instead of with the nekuia. It turns at once to nekuia, however, and then to the repeat, before arriving again at metamorphosis. This pattern is not quite like that of Cantos 1 and 2, but the separate components are much the same: The metamorphosis is a moment of epiphany or "epopte," when we capture a vision of the "Gods, etc."; the nekuia is a search through a darkness complicated by error and confusion; and the repeat involves simple repetition as well as images and allusions to guides who can lead toward light.

An image of the divine creative mind opens in Canto 116:

Came Neptunus
      his mind leaping
          like dolphins [116/795]

This is the joyfully creative Neptune from whom "Gemisto stemmed all" [83/528], and the image is a measure of splendor against which human creativity can be judged in Canto 116, where human moments will echo this glimpse of the gods.

The nekuia is most evident early in Canto 116 in the many references to darkness or error: "wrecked for an error . . . great darkness . . . madness . . . wrecks . . . voice of famine . . . blackness." Near the center of the Canto there is a moment of personal darkness:

> . . . my errors and wrecks lie about me.
> And I am not a demigod,
> I cannot make it cohere.
> If love be not in the house there is nothing.
> The voice of famine unheard. [116/796]

Then there is a shift, with the line "How come beauty against this blackness," and from this point the Canto offers counter-paths, only one of which leads to confusion. Often the paths are set side by side:

> the verb is "see," not "walk on"
> i.e. it coheres all right
> > even if my notes do not cohere.
> Many errors,
> > a little rightness, [116/796-7]

and one of the most intense images in the Canto is a quotation from Dante which sets the short day against the great sweep of shadow, "al poco giorno / ed al gran cerchio d'ombra." Thus the Canto moves from fairly constant darkness in the first lines after the opening imagery of creativity, into a more rapid alternation of darkness and light. However, very early in the Canto there is one image that is of both nekuia and of light; this is the single word, *cuniculi*. These underground canals were created by men long before the date once thought to be the beginning of civilization in Italy; so they are images of underground passageways (similar to the dromena in the rites) and yet they are an echo of Neptune's creativity. In one other way *cuniculi* suggests the nekuia; it demands from most readers a journey to history, or at least to a good dictionary, since few of us, when we first read the Canto, know what the word means.

Because both *The Cantos* as a whole and Canto 116 in particular are identified with the guide and the repeat, we will need to look at this part of the pattern more than once, especially in discussions of ideogram and Fresco, so at this point we will just identify the repeat, recalling that it is almost always a guide. Because Canto 116 is itself a tribute to Dante's *Paradiso*, we have again the use of structure as subject, the use of the past as guide in writing of the use of the past as guide, much as we saw it in Canto 1. *The Cantos* themselves are identified, in the image of the great ball of crystal, as a guide; and the palimpsest, to which we will return in the discussion of ideogram, is perhaps the most important image of the repeat in Canto 116, if not in *The Cantos* as a whole. The squirrels and bluejays are guides, and links with the divine, in Canto 116. Ariadne is mentioned, and so are specific human guides: Disney, Pound, Mussolini, Laforgue, Linneaus, Adams, Justinian. Some of these suffer from error and hinder more than they help, just as some records (a form of repeat) are more burden than help. But others of the guides emerge out of the darkness and error as moments of the "little light," human instances of divine splendor.

The spezzato light of human rightness is the metamorphosis of Canto 116 and it recurs:

a little light
        in great darkness—
cuniculi—

        . . .
Can you enter the great acorn of light?

        . . .
How came beauty against this blackness,
Twice beauty under the elms—

        . . .
A little light, like a rushlight
        to lead back to splendour.

This human recreation of divine beauty will be seen as the "answer" in the fugue pattern, to the opening divine statement; it is at the same time the Canto's second epiphany, as the human creators move out of confusion and error toward the achievement of the possible, "to make Cosmos."

Because of the Canto's emphasis on the guide, the palimpsest is a good ideogram for Canto 116. A palimpsest is a tablet upon which something has been written, then erased so that something else can be written over the original, which yet shows through. This Canto is Dante's truth made new by Pound, and it can again be made new by those who follow.

I find three main radicals to the ideogram of the palimpsest, two of which contain sub-radicals. A "little light" is the central definition of both palimpsest and guide in Canto 116, a human repeat of divine light, and it has no sub-radicals, but both the guides and the records can be subdivided.

Here is a chart outlining these relationships:

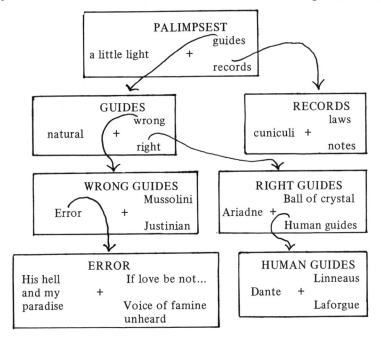

On the page, the subjects of the Canto are organized as a fugue that moves from a slow counterpoint of dark/light to a rapid motion of the same sort. The subject of the fugue is the image of the creative divine mind:

> Came Neptunus
>   his mind leaping
>   like dolphins,

and it is immediately answered by the creative human mind:

> These concepts the human mind has attained.
> To make Cosmos--
> To achieve the possible-- [116/795]

The Canto depends upon both for the theme of creativity, playing that theme against the countersubject (the false guide) and the answer to the countersubject (error), especially in the first part, down to the line that begins "How came beauty." The fugue to that point can be outlined as follows (with line numbers in parentheses):

> A: Subject. Neptune's creative mind (1-3)
> AA: Answer. Man's creative mind (4-6)
> B: Countersubject. Mussolini (7)
> BB: Answer to countersubject. Error (7)
>
>   AA: Episodes on man's creative mind (8-13)
>   "Unprepared young . . . works unfinished"

> BB: Episodes on error (14-22)
> Unprepared young . . . works unfinished"
>
> AA: Episode on man's creative mind (23-25)
> "I have brought . . . acorn of light"
>
> BB: Episode on error (26-31)
> "the madness . . . famine unheard"

Now there is a change as the pattern quickens. As we noticed earlier, the alternate paths of the second part of the canto are presented more rapidly, with dark set against light line by line or half line by half line. The emphasis on human attempts to achieve the possible continues, allowing for a movement toward reconciliation, so that although human and divine are never identified, they are brought close.

Because the concept of the guide is the basic ideogram of the Canto, the center band of the Fresco becomes the most important part of the "map" the Frescoes provide. All of the guides take on a kind of divinity because we are now near the end of *The Cantos* and because this Canto is itself a defense of the poem as link with the divine. Almost any of the guides might serve as the Fresco zodiac figures, timeless symbols of time, no longer quite human because of their awareness of the world of the gods. But in some of the guides in Canto 116 this quality is emphasized; they are presented without the casual or modern connotations we expect of the lower section in a Fresco, having instead the detached and quiet appearance of the zodiac figures: Dante, present through most of the Canto, or his image of "al poco giorno / ed al gran cerchio d'ombra," or Ariadne, or Pound's image of the great ball of crystal. Other guides, both those that lead back into error and those that are creative, seem more human and more appropriate to the lower section of the Fresco: Mussolini and his haystack of laws, for example, or Disney, or Pound himself.

The upper section of the Fresco, the image of the divine Neptune, "his mind leaping / like dolphins" is clearly presented, and it serves, as the upper sections of the Frescoes all serve, as an indication of theme, or the ideal toward which the human mind strives. The meaning of every subject in Canto 116 depends to some extent on this image.

Awareness of each of these patterns provides something that the others do not. The Eleusinian motion from darkness to light is basic to an understanding of *The Cantos*, but fugue adds an orderly sense of procession and reconciliation to the basic motion. Ideogram and Fresco both help the reader cluster subjects within the mind of the reader, but Fresco adds awareness of the gods to the basic connotations built by the ideogramic method.

Finally, the "nesting" organization of all the patterns allows for variety. This nesting of structures within structure is the one form by which all the analogies work. The basic structuring units, the subjects, are set within canto, cantos within decad and decads within the poem. The nekuia of Canto 1 is not only repeated often throughout the poem, but it is enclosed, together with the other journeys, in the macro-nekuia of the poem's overall progress from hell to heaven, through dromena to epopte. Each canto can be seen as an ideogram which in turn is composed of "radicals," which may in turn be ideograms; and these may each in turn be composed of subideograms. The decads can be thought of as supra-ideograms containing the canto-ideograms as radicals, and the entire poem is one ideogram of love, error, beauty and striving. Similarly, the subject becomes the basic unit of a fugue, which in turn is enclosed within a decad-fugue, and that within either McNaughton's three fugues, or within one master fugue. Finally, as each canto is presided over by a god or demi-god, so each decad or section has its presiding deity, and *The Cantos* as a single poem may be said to worship Aphrodite.

Because there seems to be no rigid rule for the length or number of items in each group (even a "decad" may not contain exactly ten cantos), the nesting pattern is open for change at the same time that it is orderly. It is, furthermore, one of the most obvious ways by which the world seems to work, whether we think of a tree, a nation, or a language. The pattern, however, and the others that have been studied in this book, even those suggested by Pound, are not presented here as the key to *The Cantos*, or as the structure of the poem. They are presented with the belief that an awareness of them and of the logic behind them, without a need to reduce the poem to conformity with any structure, may serve the reader as a guide to *The Cantos*.

BIBLIOGRAPHY

Two basic guides to *The Cantos* have been consulted, if not cited, many times:

Edwards, John H. and W.W. Vasse. *Annotated Index to the Cantos of Ezra Pound.* Berkeley: Univ. of California Press, 1957. [*Index*]

Terrell, Carroll F. *A Companion to the Cantos of Ezra Pound.* Berkeley: Univ. of California Press, 1980. Vol. I. [*Comp*]

Works by Ezra Pound

Abbreviations used in citations to Pound's works will be found at the left, before each entry. This list is a version of the one used in *Paideuma*.

ABCR   *ABC of Reading.* New York: New Directions, 1960.

Music   *Ezra Pound and Music, The Complete Criticism.* Ed. R. Murray Schafer. New York: New Directions, 1977.

VR   *Ezra Pound and the Visual Arts.* Ed. Harriet Zinnes. New York: New Directions, 1980.

GK   *Guide to Kulchur.* New York: New Directions, 1952.

Instig.   *Instigations*, including *The Chinese Written Character as a Medium for Poetry.* London: Faber and Faber, 1967.

EP/G   Interview with Allen Ginsberg, "Allen Verbatim." *Paideuma*, 3 (1974), pp. 254-273.

EP/B   Interview with D.G. Bridson, "An Interview with
              EP." *New Directions*, No. 17 (1961), pp. 159-
              184.

EP/H   Interview with Donald Hall. "The Art of Poetry V."
              Paris Review, No. 28 (1962), pp. 22-51.

CNTJ   "Introduction." *The Classic Noh Theatre of Japan.*
              New York: New Directions, 1959.

LE   *Literary Essays of Ezra Pound.* Ed. T.S. Eliot. New
              York: New Directions, 1954

MIN   *Make It New.* London: Faber and Faber, 1934.

LPJ   *Pound/Joyce: The Letters of Ezra Pound to James
              Joyce with Pound's Essay on Joyce.* Ed. For-
              rest Read. New York: New Directions, 1970.

L   *The Selected Letters of Ezra Pound, 1907-1941.*
              Ed. D.D. Paige. New York: New Directions.
              1971.

SP   *Selected Prose 1909-1965.* Ed. William Cookson.
              New York: New Directions, 1975.

SR   *The Spirit of Romance.* New York: New Directions,
              1968.

Select Bibliography

Adams, Charles F., ed. *Life and Works of John Adams.* 10 vols.
    Boston: Little, Brown & Co.. 1856.

Adams, Stephen J. "Are the Cantos a Fugue?" *University of
    Toronto Quarterly*, 45 (1975), pp. 67-76.

———————. "Musical Neofism: Pound's Theory of Harmony in
    Context." *Mosaic*, 13, No. 2 (1979-80), pp. 49-69.

Alexander, Michael. *The Poetic Achievement of Ezra Pound.*
    London: Faber and Faber, 1979.

—————. "Pound's Sense of Humour." *Agenda*, 17-18 (1980), pp. 122-129.

Ancona, Paolo D'. *The Schifanoia Months at Ferrara*. Milan: Edizioni del Milione, 1954.

Bacigalupo, Massimo. *The Forméd Trace*. New York: Columbia University Press, 1980.

Baumann, Walter. *The Rose in the Steel Dust*. Coral Gable, Florida: University of Miami Press, 1970.

Bernstein, Michael Andre. "Identification and Its Vicissitudes: The Narrative Structure of Ezra Pound's *Cantos*." *Yale Review*, 69 (1979-80), pp. 540-556.

—————. *The Tale of the Tribe*. Princeton: Princeton University Press, 1980.

Bridson, D.G. "Introduction to 'Four Steps.'" *Agenda*, 17-18 (1980), pp. 131-139.

—————. "Italian Painting in the Cantos." *Agenda*, 17-18 (1980), pp. 210-217.

Brooker, Peter. *A Student's Guide to the Selected Poems of Ezra Pound*. London: Faber & Faber, 1979.

Brooke-Rose, Christine. *A Structural Analysis of Pound's Usura Canto: Jacobson's Method Extended and Applied to Free Verse*. The Hague: Mouton, 1976.

—————. *A ZBC of Ezra Pound*. Berkeley: University of California, 1971.

Bunting, Basil. "Yeats Recollected." *Agenda*, 12 (1974), pp. 36-47.

Bush, Ronald. *The Genesis of Ezra Pound's Cantos*. Princeton: Princeton University Press, 1976.

Cairola, Aldo, and Enzo Carli. *Il Palazzo Pubblico Di Siena*. Roma: Editalia, 1963.

Cookson, William. "Some Notes on Rock Drill and Thrones." *Agenda*, 4 (1965), pp. 30-37.

Davenport, Guy. "Reading of I-XXX of the Cantos of Ezra Pound." Diss. Harvard 1961.

Davie, Donald. "Cypress Versus Rock-slide: An Appreciation of Canto 110." *Agenda*, 8 (1970), pp. 19-26.

_____ *Ezra Pound: Poet as Sculptor*. New York: Oxford University Press, 1964.

_____ *Pound*. London: Fontana, 1975.

Dekker, George. *Sailing After Knowledge: The Cantos of Ezra Pound*. London: Routledge & Kegan Paul, 1963.

Dembo, L.S. "Ezra Pound: Fac Deum." In his *Conceptions of Reality in Modern American Poetry*. Berkeley: University of California Press, 1966, pp. 151-182.

Dickey, R.P. "Introduction to the Esthetic and Philosophy of the Cantos." *Sou'wester*, nv, (Fall, 1970), pp. 21-35.

Eastman, Barbara. "The Gap in *The Cantos*: 72 and 73." *Agenda*, 17-18 (1980), pp. 142-156.

Emery, Clark M. *Ideas into Action*. Coral Gables, Fla.: University of Miami Press, 1958.

Espey, John. *Ezra Pound's Mauberley*. 1955; rpt. Berkeley: University of California Press, 1974.

Feder, Lillian. *Ancient Myth in Modern Poetry*. Princeton: Princeton University Press, 1971.

Fitts, Dudley. "Music Fit for the Odes." *The Hound and Horn*, 4 (1930), pp. 278-279.

Flory, Wendy Stallard. *Ezra Pound and the Cantos: A Record of Struggle*. New Haven: Yale University Press, 1980.

Fraser, George S. *Ezra Pound*. London: Oliver and Boyd, 1960.

Fuller, Buckminster. "Pound, Synergy, and the Great Design." *Agenda*, 16 (1979), pp. 130-164.

Gaisser, Julia H. "A Structural Analysis of the Digressions in the Iliad and the Odyssey." *Harvard Studies in Classical Philology*, 73 (1969), pp. 1-44.

Gibbons, Reginald. "Pound and the Gods." *Agenda*, 17-18 (1980), pp. 239-255.

Giovannini, Giovanni. *Ezra Pound and Dante*. New York: Haskell House Publishers Ltd., 1974.

Grover, Philip, ed. *Ezra Pound: The London Years*. New York: AMS Press, 1978.

Harmon, William. *Time in Ezra Pound's Work*. Chapel Hill: The University of North Carolina Press, 1977.

Hesse, Eva. *New Approaches to Ezra Pound*. Berkeley: University of California Press, 1969.

James, Henry. "John S. Sargent." *Picture and Text*. New York: Harper and Brothers, 1893.

Jernigan, Charles. "The Song of Nail and Uncle: Arnaut Daniel's Sestina 'Lo ferm voler g'el cor m'intra'." *Studies in Philology*, 71 (1974), pp. 127-151.

John, Roland. "A Note on the Meaning of the Cantos." *Agenda*, 17-18 (1980), pp. 257-263.

Juhasz, Suzanne. *Metaphor and the Poetry of Williams, Pound, and Stevens*. Lewisburg, Pa.: Bucknell University Press, 1974.

Kearns, George. *Guide to Ezra Pound's Selected Cantos*. New Brunswick: Rutgers University Press, 1980.

Kenner, Hugh. "Art in a Closed Field." *Virginia Quarterly Review*, 38 (1962), pp. 597-613.

Kenner, Hugh. "Drafts & Fragments & the Structure of the Cantos." *Agenda*, 8 (1970), pp. 7-18.

——————. *The Poetry of Ezra Pound*. Norfolk, Conn.: New Directions, 1951.

—————— *The Pound Era*. Berkeley: The University of California Press, 1971.

Knapp, James F. *Ezra Pound*. Boston: Twayne Publishers, 1979.

Langbaum, Robert. "Ezra Pound's Dramatic Monologues." *Critics on Ezra Pound*. Ed. E. San Juan, Jr. Coral Gables, Fla.: University of Miami Press, 1972.

Leary, Lewis G. *Motive and Method in the Cantos*. New York: Columbia University Press, 1954.

Leavis, Frank R. "Ezra Pound." [1932]; rpt. in *Ezra Pound*. Ed. Walter Sutton. Englewood Cliffs, N. J.: Prentice-Hall, Inc., 1963.

—————— *New Bearings in English Poetry*. London: Chatto & Windus, 1938.

Lewis, Wyndham. "A Man in Love with the Past." *Critics on Ezra Pound*. Ed. E. San Juan, Jr. Coral Gables, Fla.: University of Miami Press, 1972.

Lindsay, Jack. *Origins of Astrology*. Tiptree, Essex: Anchor, 1971.

MacDiarmid, Hugh. "The Esemplastic Power." *Agenda*, 8 (1970), pp. 27-30.

Makin, Peter. *Provence and Pound*. Berkeley: University of California Press, 1978.

Materer, Timothy. *Vortex: Pound, Eliot and Lewis*. Ithaca, N. Y.: Cornell University Press, 1979.

McDougal, Stuart Y. *Ezra Pound and the Troubadour Tradition*. Princeton: Princeton University Press, 1972.

Merchant, Moelwyn. "The Coke Cantos." *Agenda*, 17-18 (1980), pp. 76-85.

Moody, A.D. "Cantos 1-111: Craft and Vision." *Agenda*, 17-18 (1980), pp. 103-117.

Nassar, Eugene Paul. *The Cantos of Ezra Pound: The Lyric Mode.* Baltimore: The Johns Hopkins University Press, 1975.

Niles, John D. "Ring Composition in La Chanson de Roland and La Chancun de Willame." *Olifant*, 1 (1973), pp. 4-13.

――――――. "Ring Composition in the Structure of *Beowulf.*" *PMLA*, 94 (1979), pp. 924-35.

Oldroyd, George. *The Technique and Spirit of Fugue.* London: Oxford University Press, 1948.

Paideuma: A Journal Devoted to Ezra Pound Scholarship. [*Pai.*] Orono, Maine: The Univ. of Maine.

Pater, Walter trans. "The Myth of Demeter and Persephone." *Greek Studies.* New York: Macmillan, 1903.

Pearlman, Daniel. *The Barb of Time.* New York: Oxford University Press, 1969.

――――――. "The Inner Metronome: A Genetic Study of Time in Pound." *Agenda*, 8 (1970), pp. 51-58.

Perloff, Marjorie. "'No Edges, No Convexities': Ezra Pound and the Circle of Fragments." In her *The Poetics of Indeterminacy: Rimbaud to Cage.* Princeton: Princeton University Press, 1981.

Petrarch. *The Triumphs.* Trans. Ernest H. Wilkins. Chicago: University of Chicago Press, 1962.

Puttenham, George. *The Arte of English Poesie.* [c. 1570]; ed. G.D. Willcock and A. Walter, rpt. Cambridge: University of Cambridge, Press, 1970.

Quinn, Sister Mary Bernetta, *Ezra Pound.* New York: Columbia University Press, 1972.

Quinn, Sister M. Bernetta. "Ezra Pound." In *The Metamorphic Tradition in Modern Poetry*. New York: Gordian Press, Inc., 1966, pp. 14-48.

Rachewiltz, Mary de. *Discretions*. Boston: Little Brown, 1971.

———. "Fragments of an Atmosphere." *Agenda*, 17-18 (1980), pp. 157-170.

Read, Forrest. "The Pattern of the Pisan Cantos." *The Sewanee Review*, 65 (1957), pp. 400-419.

——— *'76: One World and The Cantos of Ezra Pound*. Chapel Hill: The University of North Carolina Press, 1981.

Richardson, A. Madley. *Fundamental Counterpoint*. Boston: American Book Co., 1936.

——— *Helps to Fugue Writing*. New York: Novello, 1930.

Rosenthal, Macha L. *A Primer of Ezra Pound*. New York: The Macmillan Company, 1960.

——— *Sailing into the Unknown: Yeats, Pound, and Eliot*. New York: Oxford University Press, 1978.

Russell, Peter, ed. *An Examination of Ezra Pound*. New York: New Directions, 1951.

Sanders, Frederick K. *John Adams Speaking*. Orono, Maine: University of Maine Press, 1975.

Schneidau, Herbert N. *Ezra Pound the Image and the Real*. Baton Rouge: Louisiana State University Press, 1969.

Scott, Tom. "Two Plus Two Would Equal Four But For the Shadow . . . ." *Essays on Ezra Pound*. Ed. Hugh Kenner. [London]: Folcroft [Agenda], 1971, pp. 35-37.

Sieburth, Richard. *Instigations: Ezra Pound and Remy de Gourmont*. Cambridge, Mass.: Harvard University Press, 1978.

Simpson, Louis A.M. *Three on a Tower*. New York: Morrow, 1975.

Sitwell, Edith. "A Preface to Ezra Pound." *Critics on Ezra Pound*. Ed. E. San Juan, Jr. Coral Gables, Fla.: University of Miami Press, 1972.

Slatin, Myles. "A History of Pound's *Cantos* I-XVI, 1915-1925." *American Literature*, 35 (1963), pp. 183-195.

Speare, M.E., ed. *The Pocket Book of Verse*. New York: Washington Square Press, 1940.

Stock, Noel. *Ezra Pound Perspectives*. Chicago: Henry Regnery Company, 1965.

_____ *Reading the Cantos*. London: Routledge & Kegan Paul, 1967.

Surette, Leon. "Ezra Pound's John Adams: An American Odyssey." *Prospects: Annual of American Cultural Studies,* 2 (1976), pp. 483-495.

_____ *A Light from Eleusis*. Oxford: Clarendon Press, 1979.

Tate, Allen. "On Ezra Pound's *Cantos*." *Critics on Ezra Pound*. Ed. E. San Juan, Jr. Coral Gables, Fla.: University of Miami Press, 1972.

Upward, Allen. "Method." 1925; rpt. *Agenda*, 16 (1979), pp. 122-129.

Watts, Harold H. *Ezra Pound and The Cantos*. London: Routledge & Kegan Paul, Ltd., 1952.

Whigham, Peter. "Il Suo Paradiso Terrestre." *Agenda*, 8 (1970), pp. 31-34.

Whitman, Cedric. *Homer and the Heroic Tradition*. Cambridge: Harvard University Press, 1958.

Wilhelm, James J. *Dante and Pound, The Epic of Judgement*. Orono, Maine: University of Maine Press, 1974.

Wilhelm, James J. *The Later Cantos of Ezra Pound*. New York: Walker, 1977.

Winters, Yvor. "Ezra Pound's Technique." *Critics on Ezra Pound*. Ed. E. San Juan, Jr. Coral Gables, Fla.: University of Miami Press, 1972.

Witemeyer, Hugh. *The Poetry of Ezra Pound, Forms and Renewal, 1908-1920*. Berkeley: University of California Press, 1969.

Woodward, Anthony. *Ezra Pound and The Pisan Cantos*. London: Routledge & Kegan Paul, 1980.

Yeats, William B. "Introduction." To *The Oxford Book of Modern Verse*. New York: Oxford Univ. Press, 1936.

—————. *A Packet for Ezra Pound*. [1929]; rpt. Shannon: Irish Univ. Press, 1970.

Zukofsky, Louis. "The Cantos of Ezra Pound." *Criterion*, 10 (1931), pp. 424-404.

—————. "Ezra Pound." *In Prepositions*. Berkeley: Univ. of California Press, 1981, pp. 67-83.

INDEX

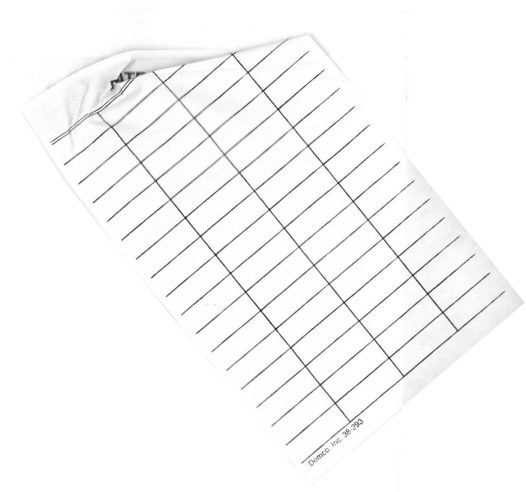

Demco, Inc. 38-293